Presented To:

_____

By:

_____

Date:

_____

GOD'S HAND ON MY SHOULDER

Experiencing the Presence of God in Your Everyday Life

HONOR **HB** BOOKS

Inspiration and Motivation for the Season of Life

An Imprint of Cook Communications Ministries
COLORADO SPRINGS, COLORADO • PARIS, ONTARIO
KINGSWAY COMMUNICATIONS, LTD., EASTBOURNE, ENGLAND

Published by Honor Books, an imprint of
Cook Communications Ministries, Colorado Springs, CO 80918
Cook Communications, Paris, Ontario
Kingsway Communications, Eastbourne, England

GOD'S HAND ON MY SHOULDER

© 2004 by Bordon Books
Developed by Bordon Books
Manuscript written by Edna G. Jordan

First Printing, 2004
Printed in the United States of America
2 3 4 5 6 7 8 9 Printing/Year 08 07 06 05 04

ISBN 1-56292-991-7

INTRODUCTION

In time of crisis, He is there. In the quiet times, He is there. When you think you're all alone, He is always there.

God's Hand on My Shoulder is a devotional book just for you, filled with personal encounters with the One who loves you most, along with encouraging reflections to help you experience His presence in your everyday life. God is always with you, but when you suddenly become aware of His presence, everything in your life changes because you are changed from within.

Read these true-to-life stories and devotional reflections to discover how God's transforming presence can offer guidance in the paths you walk, and comfort that will wipe away the tears you cry. God is also present to share with you the happiest moments of your life—because He is always there and cares for you deeply. Allow Him to change your life and your heart as He reveals himself and His wonderful grace to you.

The Lord is with me; I will not be afraid. What can man do to me?
PSALM 118:6 NIV

The only thing we have to fear is fear itself.

DON'T
BE AFRAID!

BETTY HEARD THE OTHER NURSES TALKING AS SHE OPENED THE DOOR TO THE LOUNGE. A hush fell over the room, and all eyes focused on her as she entered. "What's going on?" she asked when she saw the worried looks on their faces.

Bonnie, the newest nurse on their shift, cautiously watched the door and whispered, "Haven't you heard? Elena is now the lead nurse on this floor. We all remember her warning that if she ever got the lead position, she was going to get back at whoever told on her."

Ruth fidgeted with her cap and said, "I think we should all go to her and apologize. Maybe she'll just tell us to forget it. After all, it's been over a year since it happened."

"Are you crazy? She never forgave her own mother for not paying her back the $500 that she borrowed from her three years ago," Kristin said, stirring her coffee. "She still complains about that."

Betty listened as suggestions were made of how to avoid Elena's wrath. Take her out to dinner? Buy her a gift? Send an anonymous letter of apology?

This is ridiculous, she thought. *How can one person make others so fearful?*

Clara cleared her throat.

"I don't think we should all take the blame. Betty, you were the one who suggested we report her. The rest of us didn't think it was such a big deal. I think it's only fair that you be the one to apologize," she said.

Heads slowly dropped and the room became silent. Betty knew that everyone agreed with Clara.

"Maybe I shouldn't have encouraged you to agree with me. For that, I apologize. But I don't apologize for reporting Elena to the administrator. She had been violating hospital policy for a whole year. All of us watched the clock when she left for lunch and when she returned. But, no one had the courage to speak up, so I did. If you allow Elena to use your fear of her to get her way, you'll never have any peace."

Betty took a deep breath, squared her shoulders, and said, "I'll talk to Elena, but not to apologize. But, each of you will have to deal with your own fear."

She left the lounge and began to pray. She felt the presence of God and knew He would stand with her when no one else would.

"Father, I know You are with me and I thank You for giving me the courage to deal with this just as You did before."

Sometimes the fear of what might happen is worse than what actually does happen. Focus on God's faithfulness and his ability to bring about a good report on your behalf.

Father, You said that You have not given me a spirit of fear. You told me not to fear. I thank You for Your presence that expels all fear.
Amen.

Whatever you do, work at it with all your heart, as working for the Lord, not for men, since you know that you will receive an inheritance from the Lord as a reward.

COLOSSIANS 3:23-24 NIV

They serve best who give most of themselves.

NOT SMALL AT ALL!

HENRY DIDN'T UNDERSTAND WHY HE WAS ALWAYS ASKED TO DRIVE THE CHURCH BUS FOR VACATION BIBLE SCHOOL. This was the third summer in a row.

"Lord, You know that I give my best at whatever You tell me to do. But, I'd like to do something else this year. Anyone can drive a bus!" he complained.

I have a reason for everything I do.

Henry knew God's voice, but his dissatisfaction made him pursue the situation further.

"I've driven the bus three summers in a row," he said to Jake, his longtime friend. "I've asked to do other things, but for some reason I'm always given the responsibility of driving the bus!"

"Why don't you ask Charlie, the administrator?" Jake said. "You'd better hurry though, because he's leaving town tomorrow."

"Come in, Henry," Charlie said, shaking his hand. "Have a seat. What can I do for you?"

"Thank you for seeing me on such short notice, Charlie. I've driven the Vacation Bible School bus now for three years. I enjoy it, but I'd like to do something else. I've asked to do other things, but for some reason I'm always assigned to drive. Why? Have I done something wrong?"

"Goodness, no!" Charlie exclaimed in surprise. "I'm sorry, Henry. I thought you knew that the parents and the children specifically ask for you. They've told me you know each child by name, and you make them feel special."

"You sing, make them laugh, and give them treats. You also take time to talk with their parents," Charlie continued. "We've told them that we have other drivers, but they want you."

"But, we want you to be happy. If you'll finish driving this week, I'll get with the board when I return and see what else we have for you to do."

That afternoon, Henry saw David and his mother waiting as he stopped the bus in front of their house. David hurried up the steps and gave Henry a big hug. His mother smiled and said, "We want to thank you for praying for David. When we took him to the doctor today, the ear infection was gone!"

Henry felt tears run down his face. "Lord, thank You for this special opportunity to serve You. Forgive me for making it look small. The rewards are truly great!"

I'll let Charlie know I'm in my place—the one God made just for me, he thought to himself.

Are you looking for something big to do for God? Maybe the biggest rewards come from doing the small things.

Lord, please help me to see that any small way I serve others is big in Your sight. Amen.

Love is patient, love is kind. It does not envy, it does not boast, it is not proud. It is not rude, it is not self-seeking, it is not easily angered, it keeps no record of wrongs.
1 CORINTHIANS 13:4-5 NIV

Love always makes things look better.

IT'S LOVE THAT MATTERS

"LILA, I HAVE A GREAT IDEA FOR OUR DINNER PARTY," FRANK SAID AS HE STEPPED INTO THE SHOWER. "Do you remember that lace tablecloth that Aunt Sarah made? Well, I was thinking . . ."

Frank's voice quickly trailed off as Lila tuned him out and began to picture that dreadful tablecloth. The handmade "work of art" had been in Frank's family for generations. Frank had inherited the tablecloth when his Aunt Sarah died five years ago at age 90.

Lila knew Frank was proud of that "relic," although it was in poor condition—frayed on the ends, dingy, and musty from being kept in storage. It would suit Lila just fine if the tablecloth stayed in storage, but she would never tell Frank that.

Lila could feel a migraine coming on.

"Lord, I will not embarrass myself by putting that monstrosity on my dining room table!" she whispered.

"If you get it to the cleaners by nine o'clock, they can have it ready this afternoon," Frank's voice resumed. "Oh yeah, Mom and Aunt Clara want to drop by to see how it looks on our table since it hasn't been used in years."

He sounded so excited. "I've spent weeks preparing for this dinner party," Lila suddenly heard herself shout. "Running errands, making phone calls, and cleaning house. And now I have to deal with an ugly tablecloth, your bossy mother, and meddling aunt!"

Frank was angry as he walked from the bathroom. He wanted to yell back, and tell Lila how selfish and ungrateful she was. But one look at his wife stopped him in his tracks. She looked so tired. Frank thought about Jesus, and remembered how He always showed compassion. Suddenly, he could feel that same compassion, as though Jesus were next to him saying, *Love her Frank. Don't be angry.*

God never puts any more on us than we can bear, he thought.

"Honey, I'm sorry for being so inconsiderate. You have worked very hard on this dinner party, and I haven't been much help. I'm going to take the day off, and we'll finish this up together," Frank volunteered.

Immediately, Lila felt relieved. "And I'm sorry for that awful outburst," Lila said. "Hey, we need to hurry."

"Where are we going?"

"We've got to get Aunt Sarah's tablecloth to the cleaners. Then, we need to find a nice centerpiece for the dinner table."

How considerate are you of others? Taking time to pay attention to their desires shows love and compassion. If that's a problem for you, then ask God to help you discover ways you can show more compassion.

Father, You are love and You have commanded me to love. It is not a take-it-or-leave-it proposition, regardless of the circumstances. Please help me to always love and show Your compassion. Amen.

Do not say to your neighbor, "Come back later; I'll give it tomorrow"
—when you now have it with you.
PROVERBS 3:28 NIV

The impersonal hand of government can never replace the helping hand of a neighbor.

A FRIEND INDEED

CHARLIE LOOKED DISAPPROVINGLY AT HIS NEW NEIGHBOR'S YARD.

It's a wilderness! he thought. *Why doesn't he do something about that tall grass?*

He turned to survey his own neatly manicured lawn. Pleased with the work he had done, Charlie returned his riding lawnmower to the storage shed, and then went inside to take a shower.

Afterwards he would relax while waiting for Eleanor, his wife, to return from shopping. Then they planned to leave for a week at the beach.

His rest was interrupted by a sudden knock at the door.

"Hi, I'm Roy Greenwood, your new neighbor," the man said, extending his hand. "I apologize for not coming to your cookout. We were so busy unpacking and moving things around that we completely forgot. Some of our furnishings still haven't arrived. There's been some kind of problem that the moving company is looking into for us."

"Hey, it's okay," Charlie said, shaking Roy's hand. "I understand. We'll invite you again after you're settled. Meanwhile, let us know if there's anything we can do to help," he offered.

"I'm glad you said that. I was wondering if I could borrow your lawnmower? Unfortunately, mine hasn't arrived yet."

Charlie hesitated.

I don't know this man. My lawnmower is expensive, and besides, Eleanor bought it for my birthday, he reasoned. He quickly came to his senses.

"Sure," he said and forced a smile. "I'll get the keys. My wife and I are leaving for the beach as soon as she returns. We'll be gone for a week, so just put it in the shed when you finish."

Charlie almost gritted his teeth as Roy maneuvered the mower from the shed and headed for his yard.

"Lord, I'm not happy about this, but I know I can't refuse to help him," he whispered. He knew God was pleased.

"Thanks," Roy called. "I'll take good care of it. Have fun!"

When Charlie and Eleanor pulled into their driveway a week later, their fence was mended and had a fresh coat of paint. A new mailbox stood in place of the old rusted one. Their lawn was freshly mowed and edged.

As soon as they took their luggage inside, the doorbell rang.

Roy introduced his wife, June, who held a casserole. Then he dropped the lawnmower keys in Charlie's hand.

"We're not staying because you need to rest after that long drive. But, we just wanted to say thanks for being such great neighbors."

"No, I think we should be the ones saying that," Charlie smiled.

Sometimes our needs are met when we meet others' needs.

Lord, please help me to be sensitive to others' needs so that I'm as quick to give as I am to pray. Amen

There are "friends" who destroy each other,
but a real friend sticks closer than a brother.
PROVERBS 18:24 NLT

You can make more friends in two months by becoming interested
in other people than you can in two years of trying to get other
people interested in you.

LEFT BEHIND!

SUSAN DROPPED HER HEAD AS SHE PUSHED AWAY FROM HER DESK. She tried hard to fight back the tears she felt welling up in her eyes. It was the third time this month she had sat listening as the other women in the office planned their weekly lunch outing and did not invite her.

Lord, why don't they ever ask me to go out? she wondered. *What have I done wrong?* Susan reached for the small blue canvass bag at the end of her desk.

"Hey girl," came a voice from over her shoulder. "Looks like you're about to break some bread. You bring your lunch a lot, it seems."

It was Rachel, from accounting.

"Yeah. Bill and I are on a very tight budget these days with him in school and a baby on the way. We need to save wherever possible."

"So, where's everyone else?" Rachel asked. "This place looks deserted!"

"They all went out for lunch."

"And you didn't go?"

"No one asked," Susan responded. "They have not asked since the first week I started this job. And to tell you the truth, I'm having a hard time with it. I don't think they like me very much."

Rachel studied the look on Susan's face and could see the hurt.

"Things are not always as they seem," she told Susan.

"What do you mean?"

"Well, the Bible teaches that if we want to make friends we should show ourselves friendly. Are you doing that?"

"I try."

"What's that on the desk in front of you?"

"It's my lunch bag."

"And how often do you bring that lunch bag to work?"

"Every day," Rachel. "You know that."

"Exactly! And my guess is that the women in this office know it too. Did it ever occur to you that maybe seeing your lunch every day is a sign that you would rather not go out to lunch? Or perhaps they want to respect that you and Bill are saving money."

Susan was quiet for a moment. Rachel's kindness reminded her of God's love and tenderness.

"You know, Rachel, you're probably right," Susan said. "Maybe I've been sending the wrong signals."

Have you ever drawn a conclusion based on what you see, rather than what is the truth? What kinds of signals are you sending to those around you that determine how you are treated? You can give the right signals when your actions agree with God's Word.

Thank you, Father, for helping me not to judge people based solely on what I see. I want to learn to show myself friendly, and I will work toward that everyday. Amen.

15

When they said, "Let's go to the house of God,"
my heart leaped for joy.
PSALM 122:1 MSG

Bless all the churches, and blessed be God, who,
in this our great trial, giveth us the churches.

COME ON,
LET'S GO!

THE SMALL WHITE CHURCH LOOKED THE SAME. Beth saw
the steeple before she rounded the corner. The weather-beaten sign in
front proudly announced the church's name, pastor, and service schedule. She parked in the gravel lot and quickly went inside, not intending
to stay long.

They still don't lock the doors, she thought, fondly remembering how
Reverend Clemson always said anyone was welcome to come and pray,
anytime.

The sun shone through the stained glass windows. Beth welcomed
the warmth on her face. Such a sweet peace. She walked to the altar,
touching each pew as she went. There were scratches on the unpadded
seats. Beth remembered curling up on the hard pew with her head on
her mother's lap when she was small. There had been no nursery or children's service back then.

The hymnals were neatly tucked in the racks, and so were the paper
fans. When it became too hot, they opened the front door. There was no

lobby, so the curious passersby took a good, long look directly inside.

The polished wooden floor creaked with Beth's every step. There was a large vase of freshly cut flowers in front of the podium. *Probably from Mrs. Flynn's flower garden,* Beth thought.

A large-print Bible, opened to Psalm 122, was on top of the podium. Beth knelt at the altar. "Lord, thank You for this beautiful little church and the wonderful memories. This is where my relationship with You began. I'm glad to feel Your presence is still here. " She began to sing one of her favorite hymns.

The house of God is not only a place of reverence, but joy and excitement too. His house is a place full of His presence.

Lord, I pray that I will never take Your house for granted. Please help me to worship You with gladness. Amen.

*Oh Lord, you are so good, so ready to forgive, so full of
unfailing love for all who ask your aid.*
PSALM 86:5 NLT

Forgiveness is not an occasional act; it is a permanent attitude.

FALSELY ACCUSED!

MARCUS FELT NUMB AS HE SAT IN THE OFFICE OF THE
PERSONNEL MANAGER. His supervisor and department manager
were quiet, but the looks on their faces spelled out the seriousness of this
meeting.

Why is she doing this to me? he thought. *I hardly even know this
woman. I could lose my job, and my family. Lord, what is going on?*

Marcus wanted nothing more at that moment than to confront the
woman who had accused him of sexual harassment and ask why she
would lie about him.

Anger raced through his mind. Then, he felt a sudden peace. *Be still,*
he heard an inner voice whisper. *I promised that I would never leave you,
and I'm here right now.* It was as though someone leaned over his shoulder and whispered in his ear.

Then, Marcus remembered one of his favorite scriptures from the
Bible: "Trust in the Lord with all your heart, and lean not to your own
understanding" (PROVERBS 3:5 NIV).

"Marcus, we didn't call you in here to accuse you," the personnel manager said. "We only wanted to hear your side of the story."

Marcus took a deep breath and told them everything he remembered. He prayed for the rest of the day.

"Lord, You know I don't understand any of this, but You do. I trust You to reveal the truth, and as an act of my faith in You and Your Word, I forgive this woman who has accused me falsely."

Three days later, Marcus was back before the personnel director, his supervisor, and manager. This time, the looks on their faces were different.

"Marcus, in the 20 years you have been with this company, your reputation for honesty and integrity, and your Christian values have gone without question," the director began. "That's why it was difficult for us to believe you could be guilty of such an offense as this. But you do understand that it is our responsibility to investigate any complaints that come to us."

"When we talked with the complainant a second time, she admitted she had made up the story to get back at you for passing her over in the last promotion. She has been dismissed, and we're dropping this matter. It will not become part of your personnel record."

"Thank You, Lord!" Marcus said aloud as he breathed a sigh of relief. "You always come through."

When someone falsely accuses you, God says He will step in to defend you. Though you may not understand, your responsibility is to forgive and continue to walk in love.

Father, I choose to overlook any offense that has been shown me and to walk in love and forgiveness, knowing that You will defend me in every situation. Amen.

In my distress I cried out to the Lord; yes, I prayed to my God for help.
He heard me from his sanctuary; my cry reached his ears.
PSALM 18:6 NLT

God hears your prayers over the loudest of noises.

TURN DOWN THE VOLUME

TONI WAS SLIGHTLY PERTURBED WHEN EVERETT FINALLY OPENED THE DOOR TO HIS BEDROOM.

"I've been calling to you for the last five minutes," she said. "That music is so loud you couldn't hear a train if it went racing through here."

"Sorry, Mom," Everett said as he reached for his earphones. "I'll keep it down. What was it that you needed?" he asked.

Returning to the kitchen where she had started dinner, Toni found herself thinking about the episode. *He couldn't hear me with that music turned up so loud,* she thought.

That evening, Toni read a familiar scripture in her Bible. "In my distress I cried unto the LORD, and he heard me." (Psalm 120:1 KJV) After enduring a number of hardships, including raising a teenager as a single parent, it had become one of her favorite scriptures.

Toni thought about how busy God must be running the world. Yet, in the midst of all that busyness she knew He always heard her when she prayed.

Thinking about His love made Toni feel close to God. She delighted in talking to Him, and it made her happy to know that He loved her enough to listen.

A warm feeling in her heart signaled that God was listening as she prayed. *He is always willing to turn down the volume, just so He can hear me,* Toni thought.

"Thank You, Father, for listening to me," she prayed softly. "You make me feel so special."

When we pray, even if it's a whisper, God stops to listen. That's how special you are to Him. He hears your prayers, and is always willing to answer.

"Lord, I am so glad You never get so busy that You don't hear me when I pray. Thank You for keeping the volume down. Amen.

*Each one must do just as he has purposed in his heart, not grudgingly
or under cumpulsion, for God loves a cheerful giver.*
2 CORINTHIANS 9:7 NASB

**No one is useless in this world who lightens the burden of it to
anyone else.**

GO THE
EXTRA MILE

"WERE YOU PLANNING TO WORK LATE TONIGHT?"

The voice came unexpectedly as Carmen flipped through the pages
of a huge tax return she was preparing. With the April 15 deadline only
three weeks away, the office staff put in nearly 12-hour days, plus week-
ends, to meet their deadlines.

Not again, Carmen thought as she looked up to see her manager
standing beside her. *This is the third time this month. And tonight of all
nights! I've got to teach Bible study at church, then I've got at least another
three hours of study once I get home if I'm going to pass that CPA exam.*

Not wanting her disgust to show, Carmen forced a smile as she
looked up.

"Hi, Phil," she said. "Boy, this one is a real mess. And I can't seem to
find any of the files I'm looking for. What's up?"

"I was going to ask your help on another tax return, but it will mean
working late," Phil said. "You seem to have a knack for finding those little things that no one else can dig out."

"Actually, I hadn't planned to stay late tonight," Carmen responded, running her hands through her long, blond hair. "I have plans. But if you need me, I suppose I can make other arrangements."

I can't believe I just said that, Carmen thought, frustrated. *I had an out and I just totally gave it away.*

"Well, I appreciate your willingness to stay and help out, Carmen," Phil said. "But, on second thought, I can see you're tired. I'm sure a night of rest would be good for you. We can tackle this one tomorrow."

"Lord, thank You for sparing me from having to work another long day," Carmen whispered as Phil turned and walked away. "I am grateful for my job, and I am very thankful that my coworkers think enough of me to ask my help."

It is not always easy to give up your desires for others. But it is the unselfish thing to do. Giving is an expression of God's love. Pray and ask God to help you to be more like Him.

Father, I thank You that I am not selfish, and that my desire is to always help those in need. Help me to have a cheerful heart and always be willing to help. Amen.

Bless them that curse you, and pray for them which despitefully use you.

LUKE 6:28 KJV

Rendering evil for evil never amounts to anything good.

AN ABUSIVE SITUATION

Shelly wiped her eyes and quickly began to reapply her mascara. She didn't want anyone to know that she had been crying.

I just can't believe she would talk to me like that, she thought. *And she calls herself a Christian!*

Pray for her, Shelly heard a voice say. *She needs your prayers and your forgiveness.*

Immediately, she closed her eyes and prayed for her manager.

"What was that all about?" a voice came from behind her.

Shelly turned to see Alice, a coworker, walking into the ladies room. "I've never seen Dawn so angry before."

"Oh, it was nothing," Shelly answered. "She had trouble reading the spreadsheet I turned in and thought I made a mistake in my calculations. She was okay after I showed her how to read it."

"Yeah, but she didn't have to go off on you like that! It was totally uncalled for."

"I know, I thought the same thing. But then I remembered how badly Jesus was treated, and I thought about how willing He was to forgive those who had mistreated Him. The Bible says we should pray for people when they mistreat us, so I can't be angry with her," Shelly said. "Christians have rough days just like anyone else. We get our feelings hurt. But that doesn't mean that we should retaliate or try and get even. I'm trying really hard to learn not to be easily offended. And with God's help, I'm getting there."

After lunch, Shelly looked up to see her manager walking toward her cubicle.

"I want to apologize for this morning, Shelly," the manager said. "I was upset, but I should not have taken out my frustration on you."

"It's okay," Shelly responded. "Thank you for the apology."

And thank You, Lord, for showing me how to handle this situation, she thought.

When given the opportunity to lash out at someone, will you take advantage of it, or will you seize the opportunity to spend time in God's presence and gain His perspective of the situation?

Heavenly Father, I thank You for teaching me patience and helping me to know when and how to pray. Please Keep me from rendering evil for evil. Amen.

If any of you lacks wisdom, he should ask God, who gives generously to all without finding fault, and it will be given to him.
JAMES 1:5 NIV

For only by unlearning Wisdom comes.

GET IN THE KNOW!

"I'VE HAD IT!" SHARON SPOUTED ANGRILY. "Three years is enough. I'm not working with Kayla on another school committee! Once again, she manipulated Emily into the leading role by playing on everyone's sympathy!"

"Sharon, calm down," Becca, her neighbor, cautioned as they drove home from the Parents and Teachers Meeting.

"Kayla is annoying," Becca admitted, "but she only dabbles in everything to keep busy—to keep her mind off of Price."

"Yes, she is in everything. And she's pulling her daughter in with her and shoving the rest of us out! Well, I've a mind to tell her exactly what I think."

Becca knew that Sharon was only speaking out of exasperation. She remembered that Sharon was the one who had told her about the love of God.

"Do me a favor," she said softly as she pulled into Sharon's driveway. "Pray first and ask God's wisdom because there might be more to this than meets the eye."

Sharon sighed, realizing that her friend was right. "It has been hard for them," she agreed. "But let's face it, although you never get over the loss of a loved one, life goes on."

Sharon started supper early so she could pray before she called Kayla. "Lord, You already know all about Kayla and Emily, but I'm asking for Your wisdom so that I can understand them. Please help me say what's right and say it your way so that I'm clearly understood. Amen."

"Sharon?" Kayla asked in surprise. "I'm glad you called. I've been meaning to tell you how much I enjoyed your daughter's dance performance in the school play. She's a natural. I wish Emily could dance like that."

"Thank you," Sharon said, pleased at the compliment. "Cheryl has taken classes for two years, and has done quite well."

After a few pleasantries, Sharon told her the reason she called. Kayla listened attentively, without interrupting.

"I really have been selfish?" she admitted. "I'm so sorry that I haven't been aware of it. You see, I was always shy and depended on Price's social skills. After he died, Emily and I withdrew from everyone. After a year, I finally asked God to help us get out of our slump and become active again—more for Emily's sake. I guess I handled it wrong."

Lord, how can I help? Sharon silently prayed as she listened to Kayla. She immediately knew the answer. *I'll help her by helping her daughter.*

"Kayla, Cheryl and I would be glad to have you and Emily visit the dance class. They offer a free week's trial. If you can make it, we'll be happy to pick you up Saturday morning and afterwards we can do lunch."

"We'd love to!" Kayla answered.

"Great. Then we'll see you on Saturday."

"Thank You, Lord," Sharon said with a smile as she hung up the phone.

Wisdom never forces herself on you. She extends an invitation. Always answer her R.S.V.P. with, "Yes, I'll be there."

Lord, You know all things. I only know some things. I ask for Your wisdom so that my understanding goes deeper than the surface. Amen.

If you are unwilling to serve the LORD, then choose today whom you will serve . . . . As for me and my family, we will serve the LORD.
JOSHUA 24:15 NLT

Your success as family, our success as a society, depends not on what happens in the White House, but on what happens inside your house.

KEEP IT
IN THE FAMILY

JUST AS NO TWO PEOPLE ARE EXACTLY ALIKE, NEITHER ARE FAMILIES ALIKE. Each family is unique, determining their own ethics and lifestyle.

What foundation is your family built upon? Who determines what's right and wrong for them? Is your family stable, secure, and comfortable, confident in who they are and what their purpose is? In Matthew 7:24-26 (CEV), Jesus said that the wise person hears and obeys God's Word. They are like a wise builder who constructs his house on a firm foundation. When the rain pours and the rivers flood and the winds beat against the house, it won't fall.

In contrast, He said the foolish person hears the Word but doesn't obey it. He's like a builder who establishes his house on sand. When the rain, floods, and wind beat against it, it will fall. In your heart, do you feel your family is built on the strong foundation of hearing and obeying God's Word?

Joshua warned the Israelites to get rid of the idols their ancestors had worshipped when they were in Egypt. He told them they needed to choose whether they would worship God or idols. But, he made it clear that he and his family were going to worship and obey the Lord.

God wants your family to be a part of His family. In order to do that you must encourage your family to love, worship, and obey Him. Then, in Him, we all truly become one big, happy family.

Lord, please help me and my family to follow You with all our heart. We desire to be Your witnesses wherever we go. Amen.

The righteous are as bold as a Lion.
PROVERBS 28:1 NIV

Courage is resistance to fear, mastery of fear—not absence of fear.

TAKE
CONTROL!

CHARLENE FELT UNEASY ABOUT THE PASTOR'S REQUEST
THAT SHE CHAIR THE CHURCH PICNIC COMMITTEE. She had
been a member of the church for only six months, and had lived in the
area for a year.

"Lord, You know I've never done this before, but in Your strength I
can do it! Thank You for Your help," she whispered as the meeting started. Charlene had arranged the meeting with the Hospitality Committee
intending to learn more about the people involved in the project. She
had not anticipated the kinds of questions she would face.

"Charlene, have you considered an alternate site in case it rains?" one
person asked.

"What about activities for the older members?" another said.

"Are the activities going to be the same as last year? We want some
new games. Bingo is old," someone complained.

"Ladies…" Charlene said as she tried to take control of the meeting.
But the barrage continued.

"Is Bob going to drive the bus? I'm not gossiping, but he always wears that silly orange cap and sings the entire trip!" one lady said.

"I think we should hire a caterer this year," another said. "The food last year was horrible."

Charlene felt herself about to panic. Her knees felt ready to buckle. *Lord, what's going on here?* she thought. *I don't know anything about these people, not to mention the things they're complaining about. This meeting is out of control. I can't control it.*

Then, on the inside Charlene heard an encouraging voice. *Take courage. I'm here to help you.*

Recognizing the Lord's presence, Charlene regained her composure. "May I please have your attention?" she said boldly. "First, let's pray." After the brief prayer, Charlene resumed the meeting.

"I'm new here and not very familiar with our members," she began. "Therefore, please stand and introduce yourselves. Then you may ask your question. Do your best to keep your questions brief, constructive, and to the point so that we can stay within the time frame established for this meeting."

If you want to take charge, then you must take courage.

Father, please help me to trust You for courage to accept a task, to start it and to finish it. Only then will I succeed. Amen.

"Everyone who exalts himself will be humbled, and he who humbles himself will be exalted."
LUKE 14:11 NIV

Humility is the most difficult of all virtues to achieve; nothing dies harder than the desire to think well of self.

I AM THE ONE!

MONA HUMMED DURING THE ENTIRE DRIVE TO WORK THAT MORNING. *Tomorrow, we'll be getting off on the same floor,* she thought as she smiled at Lance. *He became a supervisor after only two years in the graphics department. I've been a writer for three years.*

Mona tried hard not to think about the 10 A.M. meeting as she sifted through some papers at her desk. At 9:45 A.M., she went to the restroom to give herself the once-over.

"Lord, You know how much and how long I've prayed about this promotion," Mona whispered. "I work hard, I stay late, and I've never been absent . . . even when I was sick. I'm the first to volunteer for our charity drives, I don't shy away from the tough assignments, and I always meet my deadlines. And Mr. Ellis said at the last meeting that my suggestion might help increase subscriptions. I deserve this promotion."

At 10 A.M., Mona slipped into a comfortable chair at one end of the long table in the company boardroom. For some reason, she felt slightly uncomfortable.

It's just fatigue, she reasoned.

Her mind drifted as Mr. Ellis discussed what many considered the mundane things—expense reports, budget cuts, new proposals. But her mind snapped back to reality when she heard the clapping.

Moments later, Sylvia Claussen stood to acknowledge her promotion as the new Managing Editor.

Sylvia Claussen? But that was supposed to be my promotion, she thought. *I don't understand.*

As she left the meeting, Mona numbly shook Sylvia's hand and congratulated her on her new position.

Later that evening, Mona pulled into her garage, turned off the engine, and sat quietly.

"Lord, I prayed for that position, but you already knew that Sylvia would be chosen. Why didn't You say something?"

In her heart He answered, *You were so busy telling Me how great you were, and what you wanted, that you never asked My will. You never gave Me the opportunity to say anything!*

That's why I felt so uneasy earlier, Mona realized.

"Lord, I've been proud and selfish," she prayed. "Please forgive me."

God already has a plan for your life. If you're not sure what that plan is, pray and ask Him to show you. If you think you know, ask Him anyway. His answer may surprise you.

Father, please help me to remember that when I humble myself,
I exalt You. Amen.

It is required that those who have been given
a trust must prove faithful.
1 CORINTHIANS 4:2 NIV

No matter how small the assignment is, be responsible.

IT'S YOUR RESPONSIBILITY!

JODI COULD HARDLY CONCENTRATE AS MRS. HUTCHINS READ OVER THE RULES AND REGULATIONS.

I've already got the job, she thought. *I can learn all that stuff along the way. I'm ready to get started.*

"Jodi, we're so glad you're here to help out this summer," Mrs. Hutchins said. "We're going to be swamped when the summer sale starts tomorrow. Donna will be very busy handling the register, but she will begin training you as soon as the sale is over."

"Today, I'd like you to put price tags on some swimsuits in the stock-room. We need them done before we go home tonight."

This is not what I had in mind as a sales assistant, Jodi thought. *Any teenager can put price tags on swimsuits!* By five o'clock, Jodi was exhausted.

Only 25 left, she thought. *I can do those tomorrow. My back and feet hurt, and I'm hungry, so I'm going home.* Jodi was headed to the office to retrieve her purse when she noticed Donna pulling a clothes rack from the storage room.

"Thank you so much, Jodi, you're a real trooper," Mrs. Hutchins said. "We needed those swimsuits tagged and racked by tonight for the sale tomorrow. If you had not finished tagging them, we stood to lose a lot of money."

Suddenly, Jodi felt a heaviness in her stomach.

"But aren't you and Donna going home now?" she asked. "It's almost five-thirty."

"Oh, no, my dear. Donna still has to put the swimsuits on the racks, and I have some more paperwork to complete," Mrs. Hutchins said, as she headed for the stock room. "But you're free to leave. You've worked hard your first day."

Jodi turned to leave. The heaviness was there again.

What would have happened to you if My Son had not finished what I sent Him to do?

Jodi knew what she had to do. She laid down her purse and walked back to the stockroom, where Mrs. Hutchins was talking with Donna.

"I still have 25 swimsuits to tag," she said. "I thought it would be all right to leave them until tomorrow. I'll do them now, and when I'm done I'll help Donna put them on the racks. Then we can all leave together."

Giving every assignment your best effort shows faithfulness. Faithfulness brings promotion. And promotion comes from God.

Lord, please help me to be as responsible with the small things as the big things. Amen.

*Always be ready to give a logical defense to anyone who asks
you to account for the hope that is in you, but do it courteously and
respectfully.*
1 PETER 3:15 AMP

Self-respect is at the bottom of all good manners. They are the
expression of discipline, of good will, of respect for other people's
rights and comforts and feelings.

MIND YOUR
MANNERS

HAVE YOU EVER BEEN APPROACHED BY A CHRISTIAN
WHO YELLED, "DO YOU KNOW JESUS?" AND THRUST A
RELIGIOUS TRACT IN YOUR HAND SO HARD IT ALMOST
JAMMED YOUR FINGERS? Or seen Christians witnessing in your
neighborhood who almost forced themselves into your home to "lead
you to Christ"? Their hearts may have been sincere, but their behavior
caused you discomfort.

When the Lord tells you to say or do something, the Holy Spirit will
guide you into the truth of how to accomplish it. He will empower you
to be a bold witness for the Lord, but you should not confuse boldness
of faith with a loud voice. It's more about the force of your faith than the
force of your voice.

The Bible tells us there were times when God spoke with a loud
voice (Deuteronomy 5:22). But He also spoke in a still, small voice (1

Kings 19:12). The Lord instructed the Isrealites differently depending on the situation. He told the Israelites to be quiet in Joshua 6:10 later He told them to shout (Joshua 6:16).

When you obey the Holy Spirit, you will do everything in a decent and orderly manner (1 Corinthians 14:40). He will be glorified, and people will be drawn to Him.

When God uses you to reach others, His voice is heard in their hearts.

Lord, please help me to be sensitive to the Holy Spirit and to others as well. I pray that everything I say and do pleases You and blesses others.
Amen.

Enter his gates with thanksgiving and his courts with praise; give thanks to him and praise his name.
PSALM 100:4 NIV

Thanksgiving creates an atmosphere where one's presence feels welcome.

ENTER WITH THANKFULNESS!

KENT TOOK TAMARA'S HAND AS THEY WALKED ACROSS THE CHURCH PARKING LOT. Everywhere, members were admiring the landscape and the beautiful new church. Even the spring weather, usually unpredictable, was perfect for the dedication.

Kent and Tamara felt the excitement and expectancy that charged the atmosphere. As they walked in, they thanked God for His love and His goodness.

"Heavenly Father, we have so much to thank You for. It's so wonderful to be able to worship You in such a beautiful new church. We look forward to Your presence filling this new one just as You filled our last one." Their heartfelt praises continued as they took their seats.

Reverend Bowman's sermon confirmed what Kent and Tamara felt in their hearts. He preached from Second Chronicles where Solomon consecrated and dedicated the house of God in prayer. He talked about how the Israelites worshipped and praised God when His glory filled the temple.

Lord, this shouldn't be just a one-time thing, Kent thought. *If this building is standing 50 years from now, we should still enter its doors praising and thanking You for Your glorious presence.*

Then, Kent thought of he and Tamara's house. He remembered the many times he had walked through the doors in a bad mood, grumbling about his job or having to work overtime. He remembered his complaints when the house had needed some type of repair or he hadn't felt like mowing the tall grass.

"Dear Father, forgive me for not thanking and praising You when I entered our house. Forgive me for not worshipping Your presence," he prayed.

When he and Tamara pulled into their driveway, his heart swelled with thankfulness when he looked at their house. "Honey, for some reason, our house looks better," Tamara said unexpectedly. "I know I sound silly because nothing looks different, but I feel almost like I did at church today."

Kent and Tamara praised God as they entered their own house. "Heavenly Father, we dedicate our home to You and we thank You that Your presence fills every room," Kent prayed.

Sometimes thanksgiving and praise at church is not enough. Take time to welcome His presence in your own house with a thankful gift of praise.

Lord, thank You for Your house of worship where I meet with others to praise You. And thank You for my house where I personally welcome Your presence. Amen.

The Lord gives his people strength. The Lord blesses them with peace.
PSALM 29:11 NLT

Like a cathedral, peace must be constructed patiently and with unshakable faith.

CALM DOWN!

SHANE AND KRISTA HAD BEEN MARRIED ONLY SIX MONTHS WHEN THEY LEARNED SHANE WAS BEING TRANS-FERRED 1500 MILES AWAY. But that wasn't all. The new company was three times as large, and he would be the director over twice as many engineers. Shane was thrilled, but the responsibilities of the new job, the move, and his role as a new husband seemed overwhelming. Questions constantly bombarded his mind.

Will the new neighbors be friendly? How can I help Krista adjust to my long work hours and constant travel? Will I fit in with my peers? How can I successfully lead this many workers? What if I fail? Where will we go? What will we do?

Shane shared his concerns with Krista, who calmly said, "Honey, let's pray. God doesn't want us afraid or stressed out. This new job is a reward for your hard work and an answer to our prayers. The Lord will strength-en us and help us do whatever is necessary."

Shane's busy schedule made the next six months hard, but God's strength and peace enabled them to make adjustments.

That following year brought a pleasant surprise.

"A baby! Sweetheart, this is wonderful!" Shane nearly shouted over the phone.

Suddenly, Shane was remembering how God had brought such sweet comfort months ago when fear was trying to get a grip on him and Krista. He could feel that same peace now. He knew God was right there with Him.

"Lord," he whispered, "thank You for our precious gift. This is something new, but Krista and I aren't afraid because we know that we can depend on Your strength and peace, just like before."

God's peace always gives you the strength to move forward. Trust Him to help you through whatever you are dealing with. His shoulder is always available for you to lean on.

Lord, please help me to rely on Your strength and receive Your peace when everything seems confusing. Amen.

The Lord says, "I will guide you along the best pathway for your life. I will advise you and watch over you."
PSALM 32:8 NLT

Everything that seems good to you may not be what is right for you.

GOOD OR RIGHT— WHICH IS BEST?

RICHARD WAS EXCITED THAT HIS DAUGHTER, TONYA, HAD BEEN ACCEPTED TO HIS ALMA MATER. His fraternity brother, who was a dean there, helped Richard make arrangements for her tuition, books, dorm—everything.

Today, Richard and Tonya were going to tour the campus, meet the faculty, and schedule her classes. *This is great,* Richard thought. *Everything is ready for Tonya. And I feel really good knowing that Phil will be there if she needs anything.*

As they drove, Richard noticed how quiet Tonya was, staring out the window while he did most of the talking. "It there something bothering you, Tonya?"

"Yes, Dad," Tonya answered quietly. "But I don't know how to say it."

"Just go ahead and say what's on your mind, honey. I'm listening."

"Okay. I really appreciate all that you have done for me, Dad, but I don't want to go to Swenson."

Richard couldn't believe what he was hearing. Spying a rest stop just ahead, he pulled over and parked the car. Then, he prayed silently, asking for the peace of God.

"Honey. Let's talk about this."

"Dad, I don't mean to hurt you," Tonya began. "I know you're excited that I've been accepted at the school you graduated from. And I'm grateful that you're proud of me. But I only applied because you wanted me to. Swenson doesn't offer a degree for what I really want to study. I think going there would just be a waste of my time and your money."

"But you'll only be studying humanities courses your first year. That will give you plenty of time to decide on a course of study," Richard said. "Surely, they have something you're interested in."

Then he felt a familiar tug at his heart. *Richard, I have the right plan for her life. Trust Me to take care of her. Just listen to what she says.*

Richard relaxed, then calmly asked, "Tonya, what do you want to do?"

"I'd like to attend community college for a year, earn some credits, and then transfer to a college of my choice."

"Well, if that's what you want then that's fine with me," Richard said. "Let's go back home. I'll call Phil from my cell phone on the way home."

Richard started the car and headed for home, assured that Tonya would follow the plan God had for her.

Are you comfortable doing what someone else expects of you, or do you desire to follow God's plan, and receive His best for you? Always make sure your actions follow God's plan. That's when success is guaranteed.

Heavenly Father, help me trust You and not be satisfied until I know that I'm following Your plans for me. Amen.

The godly will flourish . . . and grow strong . . . . Even in old age they will still produce fruit; they will remain vital and green.
PSALM 92:12-14 NLT

The year grows rich as it groweth old, and life's latest sands are its sands of gold!

OLDER BUT BETTER

GENE MARVELED AS HE WATCHED MR. HATCHET MOVE FROM ONE MACHINE TO THE NEXT; HIS STANCE AND BREATHING WERE PERFECT. His repetitions were precise. Gene returned to the bench press and began putting the weights on the bar. Suddenly, he heard someone yell, "Wait!" It was Mr. Hatchet, rushing over to him. "You're doing this all wrong. Here, let me help you."

Gene was embarrassed because everyone stopped to look at him. "I don't think you can help me, old man," he snickered. "In fact, I think you're the one who needs help," he scowled and walked away.

Gene knew God wasn't pleased with the disrespect he showed Mr. Hatchet, but he was too embarrassed and too proud to apologize.

"He put the weights on wrong," he heard Mr. Hatchet say. It was as if he wanted Gene to hear him. "What he's doing is dangerous, and he doesn't have anyone standing by in case he needs help."

"I'm going to hit the shower and get out of here," Gene mumbled. *I'll come back tomorrow after midnight, when the place will be almost empty,* he reasoned.

"How's it going?" Gene heard someone ask as he was leaving. "I'm Mark, the manager," he said, offering his hand.

"Glad to meet you. I'm Gene."

"I saw Mr. Hatchet trying to help . . ."

"Look, this is my first visit here, but I know a little about weightlifting, okay? I'm not going to have some old geezer tell me what to do!"

"That old geezer's name is Mr. Hatchet. He's 85 years old, and is our oldest and most respected member. He competed in the Olympics several times and won a couple of gold medals. My advice is that you listen to him. Just about everyone here has at one time or another. Good night."

At first, Gene felt angry with Mark. But then he felt ashamed that he had disrespected Mr. Hatchet. *Lord, you're always using people to help me,* Gene thought. *I should have realized that was why Mr. Hatchet was here.*

When Gene returned the next night, the gym was nearly deserted. He found a bench and weights and quickly put the weights on the bar. *Weights on wrong* kept going through his mind. He shook his head, trying to clear it. He positioned himself on his back under the bar, gritted his teeth and began to lift. Suddenly, the bar tilted and Gene nearly fell to the floor with the weights about to land on top of him. At that moment, strong hands grabbed the bar and weights.

"Need help?" the kind voice asked.

"Yes sir, Mr. Hatchet. I sure do," Gene said.

God has different ways of getting your attention. Staying connected to Him through prayer will help you recognize when He is speaking to you.

Lord, thank You for Your love, grace, and mercy. Please help me to always honor the "aged" for their wisdom, strength, endurance, and courage. Amen.

A gossip betrays a confidence, but a trustworthy man keeps a secret.
PROVERBS 11:13 NIV

Hear no ill of a friend, nor speak any of an enemy.

DON'T TELL IT!

KATHY LOOKED OUT HER KITCHEN WINDOW AND SIGHED CONTENTEDLY. *At last,* she thought. *We're in the kind of neighborhood we've wanted for so long. Ted and I have been invited to join the country club. Our children are in one of the best schools in this city. Thank You, Lord, for answering our prayer.*

Just then, she heard a knock at the front door. She smiled when she saw Mrs. Hinson, the wife of the country club president, standing on the porch. "Mrs. Hinson, what a pleasant surprise," she said. "Come in, please. Would you like some coffee?" Kathy asked, heading back to the kitchen.

"I'd love some, thank you," Mrs. Hinson replied, following Kathy.

"Kathy," she began, stirring her coffee as they sat at the table, "do you have any questions before we introduce you and Ted to the club next week?"

"No," Kathy answered. "You explained everything at the first meeting."

"Good. Dianne, our secretary, will call you tomorrow to get some important information for our records. Bless her heart, she's going through a rough time. Her husband ran off with his secretary. And the woman is twice his age! Can you believe that? And I've heard that she had not one, but two facelifts! Everyone knows he's after her money," Mrs. Hinson said as she finished her coffee.

"Also, Ruth, the chairman of our ladies' auxiliary, will call you tonight to discuss some of our spring activities. Now, I'm not gossiping, mind you," she said, lowering her voice as if others were near, "but the poor dear has been so lonely since her husband and son died in a car crash. Her husband was driving drunk and ran off the road. I know you won't repeat this, but she's seeing a psychiatrist. Members avoid her because she talks so much and meddles in everyone's business. Her feelings would be hurt if she knew that."

Kathy felt uncomfortable. *This is wrong,* she thought.

A familiar voice agreed with her. *Yes, it is!*

"Mrs. Hinson, I'm assuming that Dianne and Ruth confided in you as their friend. You and I are Christians, so let's pray for them, and not betray their confidence. Now, is there anything else we need to discuss?" she said sweetly as she got up to pour Mrs. Hinson more coffee.

Most likely, you have already faced the temptation to gossip. How did you handle it? Spreading gossip and rumor can cause hurt. Follow God's example and speak only words that build up and encourage.

Lord, please help me to be a true friend who prays for others—not one who talks about others. Amen.

Oh, the joys of those who do not follow the advice of the wicked, or
stand around with sinners, or join in with scoffers.
But they delight in doing everything the Lord wants.
PSALM 1:1 NLT

Let us, then, be what we are; speak what we think;
and in all things keep ourselves loyal to truth.

STAND UP!
STAND OUT!

"I'VE HAD IT!" PRISCILLA YELLED, THROWING HER
PURSE ONTO HER BED. "I'm 25, attractive, and a college graduate,"
she said, convincing herself of her good points. "I enjoy my job, and I'm
good at it. My income is above average, and I have my own home. I travel to places other women only dream of! I'm friendly, and I help others
whenever I can. I try to fit in with my co-workers, but I'm always left
out or laughed at! So, what's the problem?" she asked herself.

But, she already knew the answer.

Priscilla was tired of her prim and proper reputation. It seemed that
her Christian upbringing only caused her to be left out of everything
that appeared to be fun.

She had received Christ when she was 12. Her parents never had to
make her pray and read her Bible. She had been happy to go to church.
But, as the years passed, it had become harder to be happy. Throughout her
schooling she had not been allowed to do a lot of the things that other girls

did. Numerous things—from makeup to dating, and even driving—were not permissible until she was much older than her classmates.

Many people thought she was odd when she didn't agree with or participate in the wrong things they said and did. She remembered how she had been laughed at and rejected. Priscilla's refusal to be part of a prank today had caused the memories to come flooding back.

"Lord, sometimes I feel like living right just isn't worth all the trouble," Priscilla complained. "Those who don't have a conscience seem to have it all. They have friends and fun. They get the pats on the back. They live it up! Life seems so unfair."

You were right when you said they seem to have it all, the comforting voice said in her heart. *Don't envy them and don't try to fit in with their ways. The reward I have for you is so much greater than what they have.*

Just then, Priscilla remembered the words her mother used to console her with. "I know it's hard for you to understand now, but just wait and see. God has something wonderful in store for you. Don't try to fit in. Stand out from the crowd and do what is right!"

"Lord, please forgive me for forgetting the hurt and pain of rejection You suffered from those You loved. I love You, and I've made up my mind to always do what's right to please You."

When you stand for what's right, you won't fall for what is wrong. God wants you to do the right thing, no matter what others say or think.

Lord, I can't begin to understand the hurt and pain
You must have felt when You were rejected for the sake of the truth.
With all my heart, I desire to prove my love for You by thinking,
saying, and doing what's right. Amen.

The tongue is a small thing, but what enormous damage it can do. A tiny spark can set a great forest on fire.
JAMES 3:5 NLT

A word that is not spoken never does any mischief.

A LITTLE MATCH— A BIG FIRE!

"I DON'T KNOW HOW MANY MORE RUDE PEOPLE I CAN PUT UP WITH," PATTY MUTTERED, DUMPING THE DIRTY DISHES IN THE SINK.

Melanie sympathized, "I know just how you feel. I had a table full of bigwigs that treated me like I was a nobody."

Joyce chimed in, "The next time one of them snaps his fingers at me, I'm going to walk right past that table like it's not even there!"

"You won't do that, Joyce. You need the money just like the rest of us," Krista mocked, grabbing her customer's order and making a hasty retreat.

"Well, I was cussed out—and I can't repeat what they said," Ella whined, her eyes glistening with tears. Shocked faces turned to her in pity.

"They tip like the stock market crashed. That big table of executives from the oil company tipped me ten lousy dollars!" Grace huffed, with her hands on her hips.

Each waitress began to add her own story—each becoming more emotional than the one before. Soon, the cooks and busboys joined in, declaring that their jobs were harder than the waitresses.

It became so loud that some of the customers stopped eating to listen to the commotion.

Richard, the night manager, came rushing into the kitchen as if the building were on fire. "What in the world is going on back here? Customers are complaining about slow service and cold food! Some are saying that they can't even hear themselves talk because of all the noise in here!"

Lord, what have I done? Patty thought. *I didn't mean for all this to happen. I just made a simple statement—that's all!*

A still small voice from her heart spoke, *It might have seemed simple at the time, but it seems to be spinning out of control.*

"Lord, I was wrong to complain instead of pray. Please help me make things right."

Patty took a deep breath.

"This is all my fault, Richard," she confessed. She was aware of God's presence as all eyes focused on her. "I was angry because of how a customer spoke to me, and I complained about it. I should have come to you. I'm sorry for causing such trouble."

Richard's voice softened. "Hey, it's okay. It's been a rough week for everybody." Looking around the room, he said, "You're a great staff. If a customer harasses you, please feel free to talk with me. Be assured, your job won't be in jeopardy. To show my appreciation for your hard work, you all will have some time off in the near future—with pay!"

It is so easy to say the first thing that comes to mind. But are you prepared for the consequences? Just as it only takes one match to kindle a fire, one word spoken in the wrong way can start a war. God's way is the road of peace. Walk with Him and enjoy his steady pace.

Lord, please help me watch what I say, how I say it, and who I say it to. Thank You. Amen.

Are not the angels all ministering spirits (servants), sent out in the service [of God for the assistance] of those who are to inherit salvation?
HEBREWS 1:14 AMP

Heavenly assistance is ready at a moment's notice.

ANGELIC ASSISTANCE

DeAnn squealed with delight when she saw the diamond earrings that Wayne, her husband, gave her.

"Happy anniversary, Dee," he said affectionately. "And, that's not all. We have a dinner reservation tonight at that five-star restaurant you've been dropping hints about for the past six months."

DeAnn rushed to the bathroom to try on her earrings. She pulled her long hair away from her ears and put in the earrings. She posed, smiling as she moved her head from side to side.

She went to her closet to get the black lace dress that Wayne loved. Next, she pulled her shoes and purse from the closet and went to her jewelry box to get the diamond necklace he gave her last Christmas. She put them all on the bed and stood back admiring the ensemble. Suddenly, she realized she needed to go to the mall to buy hosiery.

She searched several stores before she found exactly what she wanted. Exasperated, she looked at her watch. *Only two hours to get ready and I need extra time to style my hair!*

When DeAnn returned home, she drew her bath. She glanced in the mirror as she put her hair in a ponytail before she got in the tub. *Oh, no! One of my earrings is missing!*

She panicked, going from room to room, retracing her steps.

When she looked in her jewelry box, something shiny in the far corner caught her eye. It was the tiny gold angel lapel pin that little Jenny, one of her Sunday school students, gave her. Jenny, who was five years old, told DeAnn it would remind her that she had an angel who was always there to help her. DeAnn smiled as she picked up the pin. It made her think of God's constant love and care.

"Father, Your Word promised that You send angels to assist us. Please send mine to show me where my earring is," she prayed.

She returned to the bathroom, and as she passed the sink, she saw something glistening in it. *My earring!*

"Father, thank You for Your help. It's truly out of this world!" she laughed.

Because you are an heir of salvation, angels were created to serve you. They are standing by to assist you at all times. Thank God for their availability and trust Him to send them when you need their assistance.

Lord, thank You for Your loving care that provides not only human help, but Your divine help too. Help me remember that angels stand by ready to help me at all times. Amen.

Everyone enjoys a fitting reply;
it is wonderful to say the right thing at the right time!
PROVERBS 15:23 NLT

A word is not a crystal, transparent and unchanging,
it is the skin of a living thought and may vary greatly in color and
content according to the circumstances and time in which it is
used.

WATCH WHAT YOU SAY!

ALL DAY LONG, YOU USE WORDS. You speak them, write them, or perhaps even sign them in sign language. Words carry power. Have you ever been tempted to say something unkind and sensed you shouldn't? God is often good to warn you not to say something you might regret.

Words can cause emotional wounds that take longer to heal than physical ones. On the other hand, words can strengthen someone to believe that they are valuable and capable.

Words can bless or curse.

Words can speak a lie or the truth.

They pronounce judgment or grant pardon.

Words declare war or negotiate peace.

Words whisper love or spew hate.

They move others to tears of sorrow or tears of joy and laughter.

Words divorce the same man and woman who were once joined by marriage vows.

Words celebrate the life of a newborn for whom you prayed, and whose journey has just begun.

They celebrate the life of a dear one whose long journey has ended.

The words of our Heavenly Father created the heavens and earth.

The Psalms are filled with words of praise for God's love, protection, and provision.

The Proverbs contain words of wisdom for daily living.

God's Word declares His great love for us in the sacrifice of His Son.

Your words confess your faith in that truth, and then God's Word declares you are His child.

Take time to choose and speak the right words. They will produce the right things in your life and the lives of others.

Lord, help me speak the right words so that You are pleased and Your will is done. Amen.

Whatever may be your task, work at it heartily (from the soul),
as [something done] for the Lord and not for men.
COLOSSIANS 3:23 AMP

Work is love made visible. And if you cannot work with love but
only with distaste, it is better that you should leave your work and
sit at the gate of the temple and take alms of those who work with
joy.

FROM THE HEART

HENRY SAT ON THE LAST PEW SULKING, WAITING FOR
THE BENEDICTION. He felt like kicking himself—again.

Why did he always volunteer to lock up the church after the evening
service? He knew it meant he would also have to pick up gum and candy
wrappers and put the paper fans and hymnals in the racks on the backs
of the pews. He would also have to sweep out the restrooms, and hang
up the scattered choir robes.

Henry looked around and sighed discontentedly. He was the third
generation of his family to be raised in this church. He really loved it,
but he wondered just how much longer he could stay.

It was a small country church with fewer than a hundred members.
However, the town was proud of it, and regarded it as a historical land-
mark. The building had stood the test of time, and withstood the threat
of being bulldozed. Within its sturdy walls the congregations had cele-

brated weddings, baptized babies, and commemorated the lives of their dearly departed. Many neighborhood meetings and church socials had also occurred there.

After the last handshake and the final car had drive off, Henry went to the basement to get the cleaning supplies and began his work. He began to hum a favorite hymn. Soon the humming turned into soft singing as he went from room to room—dusting, polishing, and rearranging. He cleaned more than he had to. He affectionately remembered the wonderful services, the precious Spirit of God, the love, the joy, the tears, and the laughter he'd experienced in this special little building.

Time seemed to fly by as Henry became lost in the presence of God. The hush over the church spoke peace to his heart.

When he was finished, Henry put away the supplies and gave each room the once-over—this time with a smile. It was as if he felt a pat on his shoulder and heard a voice say, *Well done.*

With a repentant heart he vowed to give his best to whatever tasks God had for him to do.

Whether big or small, every task is important. You honor God when you give it your best effort.

Lord, please help me to realize that whenever I do my best, I touch Your heart and others' hearts too. Pleasing You is my greatest reward. Amen.

Husbands must give honor to your wives. Treat her with understanding
as you live together. She may be weaker than you are, but
she is your equal partner in God's gift of new life. If you don't treat her
as you should, your prayers will not be heard.

1 PETER 3:7 NLT

The woman who is known only through a man is known wrong.

WEAK BUT NOT HELPLESS!

"WHAT'S THE MATTER?" HILLARY ASKED HER TEARFUL FRIEND.

"Cal is the sweetest husband in the world, but he acts like I can't think, do, or even speak for myself," Marcie answered.

"Yesterday, Mrs. Jenkins asked if I'd teach the adult Sunday School class for her next Sunday. Cal told her I was a baby Christian, and he felt I wasn't ready to handle it. Hillary, I've been a Christian for two years and, besides, we're only talking about one day!"

"Marcie, you and Cal have only been married six months," her friend said. "Be patient. He's quite a bit older than you, and he knows that you've been sheltered all your life. Even you have to admit that you're not used to handling things on your own."

"Maybe you're right. I guess he's just trying to protect me," Marcie decided. "I'm sure things will get better."

But, things didn't get better. More and more, Cal made decisions for

Marcie. When someone asked her a question or for her opinion, he answered for her. He pointed out her mistakes and corrected her. He questioned her judgment and lectured her constantly. He handled her problems. When they prayed, the only thing she said was "Amen" when they finished.

Soon, Marcie began to feel incompetent and became withdrawn. She tried to avoid conversation with Cal. She hesitated or stammered when she spoke. She was no longer the bubbly, outgoing woman he had married. Cal ignorantly thought she was learning to be dependent upon him. After all, wasn't he the good, strong, responsible husband who made everything easy for his young wife?

Besides, the Bible said the wife is weaker, he thought.

One afternoon Cal overheard Mrs. Jenkins talking to her husband after church.

"It's really sad that Marcie has stopped being active in church. She used to be so happy and energetic—a real go-getter. That's why I asked her to teach for me. But now, she acts like she's afraid to open her mouth. You would think she's abused, but we all know Cal adores her."

Are they talking about my Marcie? "Lord, please show me where I messed up," he cried. Cal knew he should talk to Marcie.

"I know you love me, Cal, but you protect me so much that I feel helpless and hopeless," Marcie explained.

Cal asked Marcie's forgiveness. From then on, whenever he was tempted to be overprotective of her, he could almost feel God's hand gently pulling him back. He learned to encourage Marcie to take control of her own life.

Weaker does not mean helpless. Instead of taking over, try offering your assistance. That's showing the love of God.

Lord, please show me how to make my strength available to someone who is weaker without making them feel inferior. Amen.

Practice hospitality to one another (those of the household of faith). [Be hospitable, be a lover of strangers, with brotherly affection for the unknown guests, the foreigners, the poor, and all others who come your way who are of Christ's body.] And [in each instance] do it ungrudgingly (cordially and graciously, without complaining but as representing Him).

1 PETER 4:9 AMP

Stay is a charming word in a friend's vocabulary.

WELCOME!

HOW MANY TIMES HAVE YOU SENSED THE SPIRIT OF GOD NUDGE YOU TO INVITE SOMEONE INTO YOUR HOME AND YOU REGARDED IT AS AN INTRUSION OR AN INCONVENIENCE? What were your excuses? Unexpected? Not enough room? Not tidy and clean? Perhaps you hadn't had time to cook.

Will the destitute notice the dust, spots, or spills? Will the blind ask what the color scheme is? Will the weary care about the size of the bed or the fluffiness of the pillow? Will the lame care if the chair is Chippendale or Victorian? Will the thirsty ask if the water is from a spring or a faucet? Will the hungry care if the plate is paper, plastic, or porcelain?

We might consider these details important, but more than likely, the one in need doesn't. In fact, none of these things even matter when God is directing your heart, and your sole purpose is to be a blessing to others.

Remember this when you prepare for weekend guests. As you are tempted to fret over what needs to be done before the guests arrive, allow God to quietly redirect your attention to what is really important.

Consider the adage: "Our home is clean enough to be healthy, but dirty enough to be happy." The only thing to add is, "Well, come on in!"

Your home holds your heart, but does it offer your hand to someone in need? If you wait until everything is absolutely perfect, you might miss the perfect opportunity to be a blessing. God desires for you to touch others with His love.

Lord, because I am your witness, please help me to keep my home as clean and attractive as possible. And I pray that I never allow pride or selfishness to hinder me from inviting anyone to be a welcome guest. Amen.

God is faithful. He will keep the temptation from becoming so strong that you can't stand up against it. When you are tempted, he will show you a way out so that you will not give in to it.

1 CORINTHIANS 10:13 NLT

It is easier to stay out than get out.

A WAY OUT!

MARTHA GAVE HER SALON ONE QUICK LOOK BEFORE SHE LEFT TO MAKE SURE THAT ALL HER SUPPLIES AND EQUIPMENT WERE READY FOR TOMORROW'S CLIENTS—JUST AS SHE HAD DONE FOR THE PAST 15 YEARS.

Walking out the door, she sighed as she read the large sign across the street: Coming Soon! Shopping Mall—50 Stores! Construction had begun, and the excited townspeople had been trying to guess which stores would be there. When Martha had found out that one of them was a salon, she had begun to worry.

Months later, after the new salon was completed, it looked like something out of a glamour magazine. It was very spacious, and had all the latest technology and equipment. In addition to a spa, they offered facials, manicures, and pedicures.

It wasn't long before Martha's clients began to cancel their appointments, obviously in favor of something new. Martha lay awake at night, desperately scheming to save her salon. She concocted ways to use shortcuts in hair care. Maybe she could use fewer products, but increase her prices.

Martha reasoned that it would not be wrong as long as no harm was done and her clients were satisfied. *It's only until I begin to profit again,* she reasoned.

One night, as she struggled to fall asleep, Martha heard a voice. *Is that the honest way out of your situation?*

"No, Lord, it's not," a penitent Martha answered. "But, I need more money. How can I compete with that new salon?"

Why do you have to compete? Maybe you have something to offer that new salon.

"Lord, I'm just a small salon operator. What can I possibly offer them? Please show me what to do." She felt peace as she went to sleep.

Just before closing the next day, Martha heard a knock. A pleasant smile greeted her when she opened the door.

"Hello. I'm Sophia, the manager of the new salon across the street. Are you Martha?"

"Yes, come in," Martha replied.

"Thank you. I've heard so many good things about you from our clients. I wanted to meet you, but I also wondered if you could help me out."

Martha listened intently as Sophia explained that she had an available room. Martha's former clients had such good things to say about her that Sophia wondered if Martha would consider working with her. Sophia explained how both she and Martha could profit. Martha agreed and Sophia left after offering to help Martha move.

Martha whispered, "Lord, You made the perfect way out for me so that I wouldn't do something wrong. Thank You."

Sometimes the best way out of a bad situation is just not to get in one in the first place. Stop long enough to think about a matter before you entertain it. God will always be there to show you the way.

Lord, please help me turn my face from the temptation and turn it to the way out that You've made for me. Amen.

Follow the steps of good men instead,
and stay on the paths of the righteous.
PROVERBS 2:20 NLT

Travel with the right companions to stay on the right road.

BAD COMPANY— BAD MANNERS

MEAGAN COULDN'T UNDERSTAND MAYA'S ATTITUDE ABOUT HER FRIENDS. She tried to respect her older sister's opinion, but this was ridiculous.

"Why are you so uptight about me spending time with Liz and Zoe, Maya?" Meagan asked defensively. "You've been like a mother hen since we ran into them at the mall last month. Why are you so suspicious?"

"I'm not suspicious. I just want you to be careful," Maya said.

"But, why? I admit that Liz and Zoe were pretty wild when we were in high school, but they never got into serious trouble. They just liked having fun. That's why they were so popular. Everyone wanted to hang with them, even me. But, they were seniors and I was a freshman. Besides, we have all grown up since then, so, why don't you give them the benefit of the doubt?"

"Just promise me that you'll do what's right," Maya encouraged.

"Maya, I go to church, I read my Bible, and I pray everyday. I haven't been a Christian as long as you have, but I know enough to stay out of trouble," she assured her.

But, more and more, Meagan got into trouble. She stayed out late with Liz and Zoe—sometimes falling into bed with her clothes on. She fell asleep at her desk at work and didn't finish her assignments. She tried to mask the telltale cigarette smoke with cologne and the alcohol with mouthwash. She couldn't look Maya in the face anymore. Guilt made her stammer as she gave excuses for not going to church.

One morning, Meagan looked at her haggard reflection in the mirror. "Lord, I feel awful and I don't even look like myself anymore," she sobbed.

She heard a voice whisper over her shoulder, *You're right. You look like the company you keep.*

"Lord, forgive me for thinking that I could stay in bad company and not be influenced." The next evening, just as Maya was leaving for Bible study, Meagan ran down the stairs.

"What's wrong?" Maya asked.

"Nothing, I just don't want you to leave without me."

"But, what about Liz and Zoe?" Maya asked, puzzled.

"I invited them, but they didn't want to come. I guess they don't like the company I keep."

You can be influenced by the values of those around you. Let God help you choose your friends.

Lord, I don't look down on anyone. I realize that there will be times when I might be in the presence of bad company, but I desire and purpose to keep good company. Amen.

Choose a good reputation over great riches, for being held in high esteem is better than having silver or gold.
PROVERBS 22:1 NLT

Strong towers decay, but a great name shall never pass away.

A GOOD REPUTATION

FRANKIE AND JADE WERE FRIENDS, BUT THEY WERE AS DIFFERENT AS NIGHT AND DAY. Frankie was a diligent, dependable, and hardworking person who did her best. She finished whatever she started.

Jade, on the other hand, was a free spirit who refused to take life seriously. She liked things easy and did just enough to get by. She always had an excuse to quit if things got complicated or hard. Her word meant little to those who knew her.

From middle school through high school, Frankie and Jade had worked in Mr. Tompkins' neighborhood grocery store. Frankie had always been prompt. Sometimes, Jade hadn't even shown up at all and Frankie did both their jobs. Frankie always kept her mind on her work even while Jade stopped to talk with friends at every opportunity. Many times, Frankie had helped Jade finish her work or discreetly corrected Jade's shoddy efforts.

Before they left for college, Frankie promised Mr. Tompkins that she would not forget his kindness and would help him any way she could.

After college, they had gone their separate ways. Frankie became an architect and Jade became an interior designer. Years later, both were called back to their hometown to be interviewed to work for Raymond Tompkins—Mr. Tompkins' son!

Frankie was thrilled but Jade dreaded the whole thing.

"I'm here because I don't have a client right now. As soon as something better comes along, I'm out of here," Jade told Frankie. "I'll quit in a heartbeat and won't look back!" she laughed.

True to her nature, Jade did exactly that. The day of her interview, she didn't call Raymond or show up. She called Frankie later to tell her she was flying to Europe to interview for the job of a lifetime. She tried to persuade Frankie to go with her.

"Raymond is a businessman. He'll understand," Jade reasoned.

"I promised Mr. Tompkins years ago that I would help him any way I could. He has always kept his word and I'll keep mine. Not everything is about money, Jade. I pray that you'll soon realize that."

During her interview, Raymond told Frankie how much his father thought of her.

"My father always knew you were going to be successful because you were honest and did your best. Before he died, he made me promise to hire both of you to design his stores."

"Stores?"

Raymond laughed at the surprised look on Frankie's face.

"Yes, Dad's dream was to own a chain of stores. I'm sorry he didn't live to see it. And, I'm sorry Jade didn't stay to be part of it."

Frankie thought of her last conversation with Jade. She saw that God had a plan when He sent her to work for Mr. Tompkins. Now, God was confirming His plan for her life.

God's Word is always good. He keeps every promise He has ever made. How good is your word? When you keep your word, you keep a good name.

Lord, I thank You for the truth of Your Word. Please help me keep my word so others know they can rely on me. Amen.

God made our bodies with many parts, and he has put each part just where he wants it. If one part suffers, all the parts suffer with it, and if one part is honored, all the parts are glad. Now all of you together are Christ's body, and each one of you is a separate and necessary part of it.

1 CORINTHIANS 12:18, 26-27 NLT

Look at the hand. Each finger is not of itself a very good instrument for either defense or offense. But close it in a fist and it can become a very formidable weapon to defense.

ALL FOR ONE AND ONE FOR ALL!

"THANKS FOR COMING, GUYS," DAN SAID TO HIS MACHINISTS. "Please sit down. I have something to tell you."

Preston, Zeke, and Eddie sat looking puzzled, holding their hard hats in their laps.

"The state laws now require that you pass a test to operate the machines in your department," Dan said. "Technology is forcing us to meet certain standards to keep our certification. We're a small company that's playing in the big league. We've got to keep up with the Joneses, so to speak," he explained.

They stared at their supervisor in disbelief.

"Dan, you know we've done this job for ten years. Production has increased each year since you hired us," Zeke said.

Dan nodded. "No one knows that better than I do."

"Besides, what can a test prove that we haven't?" Preston asked.

"I'm sorry, guys. I presented the same arguments, but, regardless,

68

you've got to take the test. I don't want to pressure you, but if you don't pass the test, there's a possibility that your department will be closed within a year. The district manager is already considering other options. Here's some information about what's going to be on the test."

Dan saw how defeated the three men looked as they got up to leave. *Lord, how can the company and I show them support?* he asked.

"Wait a minute," Dan said. "I want you to know that we're in this together. This company needs you. I need you. I want you to take two weeks off, with pay, to study. And, I'm praying for you," he said, as they left his office.

Later, the three men met in the break room. "I appreciate that Dan said we're in this together. He and the company need us and we need them," Preston emphasized.

"Let's pray for God's help for the company and ourselves," Zeke said.

As they prayed, Eddie sensed a strong presence of God in the room. He felt that God had given him a solution to their situation.

"Since all of us have to take the test, we can help each other study. Then it won't be so hard," Eddie suggested.

Each man agreed.

Dan called them into his office a week after the test.

"Congratulations! You all scored above average," he announced. "The district manager is so impressed that he's expanding the department, and making you team leaders."

"I don't need anyone!" can be the greatest cry of loneliness and the greatest plea for help. But it doesn't have to be your cry. You have God on your side, and He is always ready to help. Just ask Him!

Lord, please help me remember that regardless of how independent I might feel, I need others and others need me. Amen.

A man will leave his father and mother and be united to his wife.
GENESIS 2:24 NIV

A marriage brings families together.

YOURS, MINE, AND THEIRS

DAVID AND JEANINE HAD FALLEN IN LOVE WHEN THEY MET IN COLLEGE. David was sure Jeanine was the right one for him, but didn't want to make a move without his parents' approval.

Both of Jeanine's parents were dead. David was excited for her to meet his parents and hoped she would enjoy them and want to become part of their family.

The moment Jeanine arrived, she felt welcome. Their family's mutual love and devotion was evident. David was eager to please them and they beamed with pride whenever they spoke of him and his accomplishments.

Their family is so close. Lord, I'd love to be part of it, she prayed.

David and Jeanine married a year later. The day they returned from their honeymoon, they were unwrapping wedding gifts when his parents called. Jeanine heard David say, "Mom, you and Dad are welcome anytime. You don't need to ask, just come on over. Our home is your home. What's ours is yours."

Jeanine wanted to spend a few days getting settled before entertaining visitors.

"Honey, Mom and Dad aren't visitors; they're family," David

reminded her. "They'll be here in an hour, so let's clean up. Mom can't stand clutter."

Jeanine pushed her irritation aside and began to help. She took the crystal vase his parents gave them, and placed it on their dining room table.

"I think it looks better in the foyer, don't you?" he asked. "Mom and Dad have theirs in the foyer too."

"This is not their apartment," Jeanine muttered under her breath.

Life became a blur of inconvenient calls and visits from David's parents. Jeanine felt their life wasn't their own. "Lord, help David and I discuss this and understand each other. And, please help his parents understand we have a life apart from theirs," she prayed.

During a rare evening alone, David and Jeanine were watching a comedy on TV. "When does a duet become a quartet?" one comedian asked the other.

"When the in-laws move in!" he answered.

David stopped laughing when Jeanine burst into tears. They talked a long time. David admitted he was so busy trying to please his parents that he forgot to consider Jeanine's feelings.

"They'll understand just as I do that we have our own lives now," he assured her.

When you please your husband or your wife, then your Heavenly Father is pleased. He will show you how to keep your marriage and other relationships in order.

Lord, help me keep order in my life, beginning with my relationship with You. Help me not to take my spouse for granted, but always show how important our marriage is. Amen.

When you find a friend, don't outwear your welcome;
show up at all hours and he'll soon get fed up.
PROVERBS 25:17 MSG

To a friend's house the road is never long.

SOME PRIVACY, PLEASE!

GRACE GLANCED OUT HER KITCHEN WINDOW JUST AS LAURA LOOKED UP FROM PRUNING HER ROSES. Grace waved and quickly shut the curtains.

"Oh, no! Bruce, she saw me. I hope she doesn't come to visit."

Grace and Bruce had met Laura when they moved into the neighborhood two weeks ago. They had been in the driveway only an hour when Laura walked over and introduced herself. Laura talked constantly as she followed Grace and the movers from room to room.

Seeing the plea for help on his wife's face, Bruce had courteously interrupted and led Laura outside, asking questions about the neighborhood. She had talked extensively about her 15 years as a resident there. She left two hours later with the promise to return with a broccoli and cheese casserole.

That's the way it had been for two weeks—Laura dropping by with a casserole or a dessert, and staying for at least an hour.

"Bruce, I don't want to hurt her feelings, but I just can't take it anymore. I keep the blinds shut. I sneak out the back door so she can't see me when I leave. I nearly jumped out of my skin when the repairman rang the doorbell today. I haven't met any other neighbors because I've been so busy avoiding her."

"Honey, pray and ask God's help," Bruce suggested with a sympathetic smile.

"I will," Grace agreed.

The next day, Grace was shopping when a neighbor recognized her and stopped to introduce herself.

"Hi, I'm Pat. I haven't seen you very much since you moved in."

"I'm Grace. I'm sorry that I haven't had time to visit."

Pat laughed. "Hey, it's okay. I know why I haven't seen you. Her name is LAURA. The same thing happened to me."

"Laura is a sweet person," Grace said in her defense.

"She's a lonely busybody!" Pat exclaimed.

Grace started to agree and explain how she felt like a prisoner in her own home, when a strong presence in her heart stopped her. She knew it was God, helping her to watch her words.

"Don't worry," Pat said, heading to the checkout lane. "Someone else will move in and then you'll be free," she said, laughing.

That evening, the doorbell rang. Grace reluctantly opened the door. There was Laura, but she didn't step inside.

"Thank you for what you said about me today. I was in the next aisle when I heard Pat talking about me. It hurt, but what she said was true. I apologize for being a nuisance. When you get settled, maybe we can have a cup of coffee."

"Laura," Grace said, smiling. "Now is as good a time as any. Come in. I already have some brewing."

Good neighbors know when it's better to talk over the fence rather than walk through the gate.

Lord, please help me to respect others' privacy. I desire to be a friend who knows when to get close and when to keep my distance. Amen.

We who believe are carefully joined together,
becoming a holy temple for the Lord.
EPHESIANS 2:21 NLT

To stay fit, you cannot get out of shape.

MADE TO FIT

JEFF SIGHED AS HE RETURNED THE SUIT TO HIS CLOSET. The look on his face was a clear sign that he was disappointed in himself.

"Why the long face?" Cheryl asked.

"I'm just put out with myself right now," Jeff answered. "I thought for sure I'd still be able to fit into that suit, but I can't. Looks like I'm going to have to buy a new one before that business meeting next week."

"Come on, honey, don't worry about it," Cheryl chuckled. "You've said yourself that you had put on some extra weight. Actually, we both have. So, how could you even think that you could still get into that suit you haven't worn for at least a year?"

"I know, but you can't blame me for hoping."

The two shared a good laugh over their weight problems. But later that day, Jeff gave the matter more serious thought. His heart was convicted while reading the story of Daniel and his choice to eat healthy food rather than the rich food offered by the king. (Daniel 1:8 NLT)

Jeff thought back over his life. Before becoming a Christian, he had always felt that something was missing. No matter how hard he tried to do what others were doing, he just didn't seem to fit in. There was no peace. After giving his life to Jesus Christ, Jeff understood why. Like all of humanity, Jeff was created to live his life with God. He was tailor-made to fit the image of God and to experience a heavenly relationship that the world could not offer.

As long as he stayed connected to God, Jeff realized, he would always fit. Closing his Bible, Jeff walked across the room and glanced at himself in the mirror. He felt God's gentle nudge prompting him to take action.

That suit was tailor-made to fit me, he thought, looking once again at his bulging stomach. *I got so busy with my work that I let myself go. Now, I'm going to have to work at reshaping myself to fit the suit.*

Jeff decided he would talk with Cheryl, and together they would work to get their bodies back into shape.

A tailor-made suit is shaped and contoured to fit one person. It only stops fitting when that person gets out of shape. That's how God made you—in His image and likeness. You are perfectly designed to connect with God.

Father, I am thankful that everyday I sense Your presence. That lets me know that You and I are fitted together as one. Amen.

If you start thinking to yourselves, "I did all this. And all by myself.
I'm rich. It's all mine!" – well, think again. Remember that God . . .
gave you the strength to produce all this wealth.
DEUTERONOMY 8:17-18 MSG

No matter what accomplishments you achieve, somebody helps
you.

DON'T TAKE
THE CREDIT!

CARLOTTA WALKED INTO HER CLOSET AND LOOKED
AROUND, ADMIRING HER WARDROBE—YOU NAME IT, SHE
HAD IT. Everything was beautiful and expensive. So were her condo,
the furniture, and her car.

As senior fashion designer for one of the top companies in the
world—the crème de la crème of fashion—her creations demanded top
dollar. She smiled as she remembered the vow she made as a child, "One
day, I'm going to be rich!"

But her pleasant thoughts were intruded upon by bitter memories of
poverty. She shook her head, in hopes of shaking them off.

She could hear her dad bellowing complaints about his meager pay
and her mom crying because there wasn't enough food. She still felt the
darkness crowd her as she completed her homework by candlelight
because the electricity had been turned off. She still heard the laughter of
her classmates as they pointed to her faded clothes and worn-out shoes.

She could see the sneers on their faces as she took her cold lunch out of its greasy bag and ate alone. And she remembered how she never invited anyone to visit because she was too embarrassed about the run-down house her family lived in.

Carlotta remembered how she immersed herself in schoolwork to compensate for the loneliness and despair. She was rewarded with honors and certificates of scholastic achievement. When she was a high school senior, she was offered a full scholarship to a prestigious school of fashion design. Before she received her degree, the company she currently worked for had hired her.

"Look at me now," she said, twirling around. "I did exactly what I said I would do. I worked long and hard and I made it to the top. I am rich! I did it. No one can take the credit for it!" she shouted.

You're absolutely right. You already took the credit for it, so no one else can! Carlotta stopped and caught her breath. She hadn't heard that familiar voice in a long time. She recognized it as the same voice that had comforted her many times in the past when she prayed for her family and when she asked for help as she studied for an exam.

"Lord, I'm so sorry. Please forgive me for forgetting Your love and Your faithfulness. Only You deserve the praise and the credit for all these wonderful things. I won't forget again," she said, with tears on her cheeks

---

Are you quick to say, "I did it," or do you give credit to the One who really deserves it?

Lord, please help me to remember that no matter how hard and how long I work at anything, I am to praise You for the good that comes from it. Amen.

Tell the truth to each other.
ZECHARIAH 8:16 NLT

Honesty is the cornerstone of character.

JUST BE HONEST

Veronica stared at the two watches laying side by side in the display case. She had come to this jewelry store once a week for an entire month, just to look at them. The silver one with her birthstone cost $299. The gold one with diamonds was $100 more. She had saved so that at the end of the month, she could buy either one.

Today was the day, and Veronica had rushed to the store to make her purchase. Cindy, her best friend, had tagged along.

At the far end of the counter, the manager talked to a new sales clerk who was changing price tags on the watches.

While they waited Cindy asked, "Okay, time's up. Which one are you going to buy?"

"I guess I'll buy the gold one. It'll go perfectly with the earrings I bought last Christmas," Veronica replied.

The manager saw Veronica and Cindy waiting. The clerk quickly walked over to them. "May I help you?"

"Yes, may I hold that watch with the diamonds on it?" Veronica asked, pointing to it. She tenderly rubbed her finger over it when suddenly, her mouth dropped open.

"$199.99!" she almost yelled, looking at the price tag. "Are you sure this price is correct?" Veronica asked.

The clerk assured her that it was correct.

Veronica wrote a check while the clerk finished the sale. When they were back in her car, she looked at the watch again. Something caught her eye. It was another tag, caught in the clasp. "There are two tags on this watch. This one has $399.99 on it. Something is wrong."

"Didn't you ask her if $199.99 was the correct price?" Cindy said.

"Yes, but . . ."

"And, didn't she say it was correct?"

"Yes, but . . ."

"You didn't do anything wrong. You're not to blame for her mistake. Just consider it a blessing in disguise," Cindy reasoned.

Veronica felt pangs of guilt. She could almost hear the voice of God. *I sent My Son to tell the world the truth. Will you do any less?* the gentle voice asked.

"Cindy, I've got to return this and tell the clerk what happened, for her sake and mine," she said. "That's the only truthful thing to do."

"You saved my job," the clerk said, as she rang up the sale again.

"The $199.99 tag was supposed to be put on the silver watch because it's on sale. Today is my first day, and I was so nervous that I put it on the gold one by mistake. I can't thank you enough. You're a godsend."

Veronica smiled.

It usually takes more courage to tell the truth. The Greater One in you is truth. Let Him lead you when it comes to speaking what is right.

Lord, Your Word is truth. You never lie so neither must I. Please help me to be truthful in every way. Amen.

SEE WHAT [an incredible] quality of love the Father has given (shown, bestowed on) us, that we should [be permitted to] be named and called and counted the children of God!
1 JOHN 3:1 AMP

I don't know who my grandfather was; I am much more concerned to know what his grandson will be.

JUST LIKE MY FATHER!

TOM STRAIGHTENED HIS TIE AS HE WAITED FOR THE COUNSELOR TO FINISH TALKING. He had prayed and waited for this day for five years. He was finally going to meet his biological father for the first time.

Look at me, he thought. *I'm 30 years old, but I'm as nervous as a young kid about to be adopted.* He couldn't help but grin at that thought.

"Tom, here's your father's phone number and address," the counselor said, handing him a slip of paper. "I hope everything works out for all of you. Keep in touch and let me know how everything is going."

"I will. Thank you for all your help. I'm quite sure we'll be just fine," Tom said, vigorously shaking her hand.

Tom prayed as he drove. "Heavenly Father, I love You. Thank You for loving me and calling me Your son. I'm so glad that You and I know one another. There was a time when I was a stranger to You, but that didn't stop You from loving me. Every day I pray to be more like You.

That's what every true son desires—to be just like his father. I'm about to meet a man who is my natural father. He's a stranger, but I want to know him and learn to love him—just like You did me."

Tom glanced at the address again. "Here it is," he said, pulling into the driveway. He took a deep breath and rang the doorbell. A lady with a kind face and warm smile answered the door. Tom figured she was his father's wife, according to the description the counselor gave him.

"Hello. I'm . . . ," he started to say.

"Oh, my goodness!" she interjected. "You look just like your father."

Yes, I do, Tom thought as he felt a warm unseen presence. *I'm just like Him!*

Do you look just like your Heavenly Father? Do others see the spiritual resemblance? When you spend time with Him in His presence you become more like Him.

Lord, I pray to live according to Your will daily so that others will recognize that I am truly Your child. Amen.

*"The Lord doesn't make decisions the way you do!
People judge by outward appearance, but the Lord looks at a person's
thoughts and intentions."*
1 SAMUEL 16:7 NLT

Beauty is altogether in the eye of the beholder.

LOOK AGAIN!

IT WAS ELEVEN O'CLOCK WHEN BETH WALKED IN THE DOOR FROM WORK. She trudged up the stairs to check on her children. She thought they would be in bed, but they were in the family room watching TV. "What are you doing up this late on a school night?" she asked.

"Hi, Mom," Josh smiled. "We were about to turn off the TV when we saw this commercial about a Mother's Day contest."

"It's sponsored by a chocolate candy company in New York," Julie explained, happily.

Beth was puzzled. "What does that have to do with you not being in bed?"

"Nothing, but we want to enter you in the contest, Mom," Josh said.

Beth stifled her laugh when she saw the serious looks on their faces. "I love you for thinking that much of me, but take a real close look," she said, holding her arms out to the side and slowly turning around. "I'm overweight, I wear braces, and I have these," she said, gently rubbing the scars on her face. "I'm sorry, kids, but I'm not pretty enough for that contest."

"But, Mom, you don't understand . . ." Josh tried to explain.

"That's enough, now," Beth interjected. She gave them a hug and kisses to appease their disappointment, and sent them off to bed.

As she lay in bed, regrets and self-pity crowded her mind. "Lord, I remember when I was the prom queen candidate and a cheerleader. I was pretty until I was burned in the science lab. I suffered because of something that wasn't my fault!" she lamented.

Beth felt remorse immediately after speaking those words. It was as though she could hear the chastisement of the Lord. *No, the fire wasn't your fault. But, if you let your physical scars ruin your inner beauty, you are at fault. The real you is on the inside.*

Beth fell asleep pondering what the Lord said.

The next morning, Josh and Julie walked into the kitchen and stared at Beth in disbelief. It was her day off, but she was dressed, her hair was styled, and she wore makeup. Beth hummed as she served their breakfast. "The Lord helped me understand inner beauty," she said, as she sat down. "I was so busy looking at what was wrong on the outside that I didn't see the good inside."

"Mom, that's why you're pretty, because you're you! You're the one who's ashamed of your looks. When we look at you, we don't see any of that stuff. Besides, this contest is not about looks. It's about what makes you a great mother." Josh exclaimed, as Beth squeezed him tight.

The phrase 'What you see is what you get!' is a shallow description of beauty. Sometimes, what you don't see is much more important than what you view in the mirror. See yourself from God's perspective.

Lord, thank You for creating inner beauty as well as outer beauty. Please help me to recognize and appreciate them both. Amen.

Put on all of God's armor so that you will be able to stand firm against all strategies and tricks of the Devil.
EPHESIANS 6:11 NLT

The least important is the most important when it's needed.

SUIT UP!

"JoAnn," George called from the hall closet. "Where are our helmets? I found the skates, kneepads, elbow pads, and the wrist guards. I thought you put everything in here after the skating lesson last week."

"I thought I did," JoAnn replied. "Look in the garage. Maybe they're hanging on the bike rack."

George looked in the garage for a few minutes. "They're not there either," he said, frustrated. "We can't leave until we find them. We have to wear them when we ride the bikes and when we skate."

JoAnn joined George in the garage to help look. "Look," she said, "we've been bikers for years and haven't always worn helmets. They just made it a law last year anyway. We've only got to ride about five minutes to the rink, and then we'll be inside. We'll be fine. We've always been very careful."

George looked at the clock. They had agreed to meet their friends, Jay and Betty, at the rink in 30 minutes. *JoAnn's right. We are experienced bikers. We've never had an accident or been hurt,* he reasoned. *Anyway, we'll be there in no time.*

George felt uncomfortable, but he disregarded his feelings. "Okay, let's go. At least we've got the pads and the guards. But, we've got to find the helmets before the next lesson," George emphasized.

They prayed before they left. JoAnn noticed that George specifically asked for divine protection—from their heads to their feet. He seemed nervous, almost uncertain about something.

They packed their gear in the saddlebags on their bikes, mounted them and pedaled to the corner.

While waiting for the traffic light to change, George seemed to feel a hand gently pull him back. *George, you put on your spiritual armor when you prayed, but you don't have all your physical armor,* he heard an inner voice say. *A soldier needs each piece of his armor in place so that he is fully protected and prepared. Only then is he confident. Are you?*

"No, Lord," he said, quietly. "I'm not confident because we're not fully prepared or protected. Thank You for warning us. Forgive me for being insensitive to what I know is right and for breaking the law."

"JoAnn," he called to his wife, "God has warned us to go back now and find our helmets. I'll call Jay and Betty. They'll understand."

Enemies can be seen or unseen. It's wise to prepare for both.

Father, thank You for being so wise to provide spiritual and natural armor for me. Help me to be aware of all enemies—unseen and seen.
Amen.

Dear friends, if our hearts do not condemn us, we have confidence
before God.
1 JOHN 3:21 NIV

I plowed "perhaps," I planted "If" therein, and sadly harvested "It
Might Have Been."

DON'T TAKE A GUILT TRIP

CRAIG WALKED THE HOSPITAL CORRIDOR, ANXIOUSLY WATCHING THE CLOCK. "How much longer before someone comes to let us know how Andy's doing?" he said.

"Honey, the doctor told us it would take awhile because they're doing extensive tests to be sure Andy's okay," Janeen replied. "We've prayed and now we must trust God," she encouraged.

" I know all that, but I still feel that I should have known that Todd wasn't experienced enough to let Andy ride on the back of that motorcycle, even if he felt that he was."

Janeen's mother wiped her red eyes. "I don't understand why you and Craig didn't drive them to the concert, Janeen. Why did you allow them to ride that thing that far away? Your father and I would never have allowed it. What were you thinking?" she said, wiping away fresh tears.

"Well, how do you think I feel?" Craig's father asked. "I thought Todd was old enough to be responsible with a motorcycle. I would never have bought the thing, Craig, if you had told me not to. Why didn't you say something to stop me?"

Suddenly, Todd jumped up and yelled, "Will all of you just shut up! I'm the one who's to blame for everything. I never should have asked for a motorcycle. I should never have let him get on it. I could have stopped him, but I didn't. I'm his older brother and he trusted me. None of this would have happened if it weren't for me," he sobbed.

"Lord, please help us," Janeen prayed. "The blame and guilt are tearing us apart," she whispered. Janeen was quiet. She needed the peace and comfort that only God could give at a time like this. She sensed His peace as she stared out the window, watching the clouds roll freely across the sky.

I don't condemn. My grace and mercy freely forgive, she felt a voice say. Janeen squared her shoulders and faced her family. "Enough!'" she said calmly. "God is not blaming us or condemning us, and neither will we. His grace and mercy are upon Andy and us."

Just then, the doctor came through the door. "We've completed the preliminary tests, and there appears to be some minor damage to Andy's spinal column," he told the family. "It will take some time, but because Andy is in such good health otherwise, we have no reason to believe he won't make a full recovery."

Relieved at the news, the family asked to see Andy.

"I'm really sorry, little brother," Todd said as he stood over Andy's bed. Andy was asleep, but as Todd sensed the presence of God in the room, he could hear his baby brother saying, "Hey, Todd, it's okay. I don't blame you. I forgive you."

Guilt trips can be very lonely. Ask God to be your companion when you need to travel.

Lord, I'm thankful that You don't condemn me regardless of how guilty I might feel. You forgive me and make me free from condemnation and guilt. Amen.

*Behold, how good and how pleasant it is for brethren
to dwell together in unity!*
PSALM 133:1 AMP

All your strength is in your union, all your danger is in discord.

WE CAN DO IT!

SPECTATORS GATHERED AROUND THE LARGE MUDDY
HOLE, WAITING FOR THE SPRING FESTIVAL'S MOST POPULAR
EVENT—THE TUG-OF-WAR CONTEST. Any team or club could
compete, and the winners received $3,000 for their favorite charity.

The local fitness club had reigned as champions for five consecutive
years. This year the tennis club opposed them. It seemed to be over
before it began. The fitness club pulled with little effort as the tennis
club toppled into the mud. The fitness club flexed their muscles and
posed amid cheers and whistles.

Charlie, the chess club president, watched the fitness members and
thought, *it would be an awesome upset for us to win next year.*

He turned to Joe, his closest friend, and said: "Wouldn't it be great
for the chess club to beat them next year? I believe that the Lord will
help us."

Joe stared at him as if he'd lost his mind. "But, they're not all
Christians, Charlie."

"Don't worry about that. Let's get all the guys together for a meeting
later today at the clubroom," Charlie said.

That night the chess club members were still laughing about the contest when Charlie walked in with someone. "Thank you for coming. Please sit down. I'd like to introduce Brad. We work together at the refinery."

Thinking Brad was there to join the club, the members rose to welcome him. "Brad is a professional bodybuilder," Charlie explained. "He's agreed to be our personal trainer and help us prepare for next year's contest. With God's help, we're going to beat the fitness club."

Charlie laughed at the shocked faces, turned to Brad and said, "You've got a captive audience, so tell us how we're going to do it."

Brad's enthusiastic plans stirred up the chess club. At the end of the meeting, they were shouting, "We can do it! We will win!" This became their motto. Whenever they saw each other, they encouraged each other with high-fives.

The day finally arrived. The chess club gathered for prayer and last-minute instructions before they marched to face the fitness club. At the referee's first signal, both teams picked up the rope. Charlie, who was the lead, felt a firm touch on his shoulder. "Thank You, Lord."

At the second signal, both clubs pulled. The fitness club became fearful when the chess club didn't budge. Instead, one by one, the fitness club members fell into the mud. A loud roar of applause and laughter heralded the chess club's victory. They gave more high-fives as they shouted, "We did do it! We won!"

Teammates can make the victory all the sweeter. There is no greater assurance than to know that God is on your side and you're a part of the eternal, winning team.

Lord, thank You for the support of others and for the success we share in joint endeavors and accomplishments. Amen.

Wives, be subject (be submissive and adapt yourselves) to your own husbands as [a service] to the Lord.
EPHESIANS 5:22 AMP

The surest plan to make a man is, think him so.

SUBMISSION AND HONOR

"BRENT, HURRY UP!" DAPHNE DEMANDED AS SHE SET THE POUND CAKE ON THE BACKSEAT OF THE CAR. "Pastor asked everyone to be on time. He's very busy, and we have to respect his schedule."

Brent rushed out of the house, buttoning his shirt while clenching a sandwich between his teeth, his necktie still untied.

He quickly sat in the driver's seat and plopped the sandwich in her lap.

"Sorry, Dee. I had to iron my shirt. Did you forget that I asked you to do it for me? Remember, I'm working late this week. And I guess you didn't have time to cook either," he said, pitifully.

"No, I didn't have time. I finished the report Pastor needs for tonight's meeting. And I made this cake for the bake sale tomorrow. Take this messy sandwich," she said, shoving it at him.

"By the way, Dee, I was wondering if you would bake a pound cake for my office party this Friday," he said, shoving the sandwich into his mouth. "They're still talking about your blue ribbon that you won for it at the state fair last year," he said, with a hint of pride in his voice.

"Brent, that's only two days away. I'll be busy with the bake sale and then the church picnic. And you're asking me to bake a cake for your office, too?"

"Sorry, Dee," he mumbled.

In the parking lot, Daphne told Brent to bring the report in while she hurried inside with the cake. Inside, she saw the pastor's wife smiling and talking to him while she straightened his tie before the meeting. While he talked with some church members, she took papers out of his briefcase and arranged them on the lectern. Finally, she placed a pitcher of cold water and a glass nearby. She seemed to enjoy helping him.

Daphne saw Brent looking for her. He struggled to carry her report and tried to smooth his poorly ironed shirt and wrinkled tie. Both had mustard stains from the sandwich.

Then Daphne looked at their pastor who was neatly dressed and whose wife seemed to adore him as she patiently sat close by ready to help if he needed her.

Instantly, she felt shame for the way she had treated Brent. She knew the Lord had caused her to look up in order to see the relationship between the pastor and his wife. "Lord, please forgive me for honoring our pastor more than my husband," she prayed with a heavy heart.

After the meeting, the pastor asked Daphne to bake a cake for the luncheon at his country club on Friday. "Pastor, I'm sorry, but I've got to bake a cake for my husband. I'll be glad to bake one for you next time," she said. She smiled at Brent and took his hand.

Your Heavenly Father is honored when you honor your husband.

Lord, I pray that my husband will know how dear he is to me as I give him a special place of honor. I believe this pleases You and honors You as well. Amen.

The vision is yet for an appointed time . . . it will not deceive or disappoint. Though it tarry, wait [earnestly] for it, because it will surely come.
HABAKKUK 2: 3 AMP

Why only see your present when you can dream your tomorrow?

KEEP LOOKING!

BRENDA AND SHEILA SAT SIPPING COFFEE AND EATING THE WARM COFFEECAKE THAT SHEILA HAD BAKED.

"This is delicious, Sheila," Brenda said, reaching for another slice. She noticed that the sliver on Sheila's plate only had a bite taken out of it. "Are you okay? You've hardly touched your coffeecake."

"I'm fine," Sheila assured her. "I don't eat like I used to because I saw a pretty swimsuit at the mall that I really want. Once a week I go look at it for inspiration. I've only got five pounds to lose and then I'll buy it. I've been exercising too, and I've lost several inches around my waist," Sheila said, as she got up to model for Brenda.

She is slimmer. Why haven't I noticed it? Brenda asked herself. *Probably because I've been too busy looking at the pie, cake, and ice cream I've been shoveling into my mouth!*

Brenda felt embarrassed as she looked at the coffeecake on her plate. She pushed it aside and tried to share her friend's excitement.

As soon as Brenda returned home, she went to her closet. Pushed to the back was a long beautiful red dress she had bought to wear to her office Christmas party two years ago. The price tag was still attached. She remembered the emergency surgery that caused her to miss the party. Even worse, the slow recovery had confined her to bed and caused her to gain weight.

"Lord, I need Your help. I've got nine months to get in shape for the office Christmas party. Any suggestions?" she asked and laughed at herself.

Suddenly, Brenda remembered that Sheila had focused on the swimsuit for inspiration. She felt God wanted her to change her focus as well.

Instead of focusing on junk food, I'll visualize how pretty I'll look in my dress. And for even more inspiration, I'll find a calendar and circle the date of the party in bold red and put it on the front of my refrigerator. "Lord, please help me be patient as I change my habits. I know it's not going to happen overnight."

Whenever Brenda was tempted to eat junk food or not exercise, she felt a gentle nudge encouraging her to take her dress out of the closet and look at it.

The night of the party finally arrived. She took her dress out of the closet, but this time she put it on. When she looked in the mirror, she didn't have to visualize. This time she actually saw a vision of loveliness.

Goals are much easier to reach when you keep them in sight. Ask God to reveal His plan for your future, and then trust Him to show you strategic ways to keep that vision in sight.

Lord, please help me to see with Your eyes, for then I won't place limitations on You, on others, or on myself. Amen.

*For the sake of Christ, I am well pleased and take pleasure in infirmi-
ties, insults, hardships, persecutions, perplexities and distresses; for
when I am weak [in human strength], then am I [truly] strong (able,
powerful in divine strength).*
2 CORINTHIANS 12:10 AMP

O, do not pray for easy lives. Pray to be stronger men.

YOU ARE NOT
A WEAKLING

TIM LOOKED AT THE TOWERING, FANCY, BRICK-AND-
GLASS BUILDING SURROUNDED BY TALL TREES AND THE
RELAXING COURTYARD WITH ITS EXOTIC PLANTS AND CAS-
CADING WATERFALLS. Tables and chairs, shadowed by huge umbrel-
las, dotted the well-manicured lawn. It could pass as a resort, but Tim
wasn't a pampered tenant on his way to a leisurely dip in the pool.

Jean, his wife, pushed him across the crosswalk trying not to let his
wheelchair bump the curb. While she chattered about the beautiful
flower gardens and landscaping, Tim's focus was on the patients who
were on walkers, crutches, and canes and in wheelchairs, assisted by
attendants and aides.

A smorgasbord of cripples—in all shapes, sizes, and colors, he thought to
himself.

Jean pushed Tim through the large double doors and up to the reg-
istration desk. The receptionist asked his name and made a brief call.
Soon, the elevator doors opened and a strong young man appeared. He
introduced himself as Jason and gave Tim a firm handshake. Jean gave

Tim a peck on the cheek and left him in Jason's care.

Jason guided Tim into a large room filled with many types of machines and equipment. Patients were being coached to stand, walk, stretch, and lift. Some cried as they attempted the simplest movements.

God, I can't do this, Tim thought. *I'm not strong enough yet.*

"Tim, we're going to put you on this table and massage your muscles first. Then we'll work up to slow, simple exercises to help you remember how it feels to flex. This will build up strength."

Tim panicked. "I can't even do the easy exercises in bed like the doctor told me. I'm just too weak. Maybe it's too soon."

"Tim, trust me," Jason said, looking him in the face. "You can do this."

"I told you I can't! You weren't the one in that car accident, and you're not the one sitting in this wheelchair!" Tim yelled.

"Three years ago, I was hit by a drunk driver, and I was the one sitting in a wheelchair, and I felt the same way you do. If it had not been for the strength of God, I wouldn't have made it."

Tim stared at Jason, speechless.

I am your strength just like I was Jason's, God's comforting voice spoke into his heart. Tim let Jason lift him from the wheelchair and put him on the table.

Jason smiled, patted Tim on the back and said, "Let's get started."

Tim prayed, "Heavenly Father, thank You for Your divine strength that overcomes my physical weakness."

Do you give up easily when it seems like a task is too much for you to tackle? God's supernatural strength and capability is always available to override your natural feelings of weakness and incapability.

Lord, regardless of how weak I might feel, help me to know that I can do all things through Your strength. Amen.

I'm not trying to be a people pleaser! No, I am trying to please God.
GALATIANS 1:10 NLT

He is rich or poor according to what he is, not according to what he
has.

YOU ARE
SOMEONE!

SHAWNA STARED AT HER REFLECTION IN THE MIRROR,
FROM HER HAIR DOWN TO HER FEET. The mousy brown hair
and wild eyebrows emphasized her pale complexion in a very unattrac-
tive way. Her year-old twin sons had helped add unwanted pounds to
her small frame. Her nails were chipped, her hands were chapped, and
her feet were calloused.

"I look like a country bumpkin, not the wife of a company district
manager," she complained. "I'll never impress those ladies. The luncheon is just two days away."

Jake, her husband, had recently joined the men's chess club. It was
understood that the wives of chess club members be invited to join the
garden club.

Shawna was concerned. Her only gardening experience had been on
their 500-acre farm. News of their unexpected twins prompted them to
sell the farm and move to this wealthy suburb.

The day before the luncheon, Jake gave Shawna free rein with their
checkbook and offered to sit with their sons while she spent the day at

the salon for a makeover.

The day arrived to meet the ladies and Shawna got dressed. Afterwards, she practiced smiling and walking in front of her full-length mirror. Satisfied with Jake's whistle of approval, she picked up her purse and car keys and headed for the door. She turned the key to the luxury car she had leased for the day, and backed out of the garage.

"Lord," she prayed, "these ladies are rich and sophisticated and I'm just a country girl. Please help them like me and accept me. I want to fit in." She felt uneasy, but figured it was the jitters.

The parking valet took the car and Shawna walked through the covered walkway to the double doors. In the foyer, Shawna noticed a group of women about her age.

Shawna took a deep breath, forced a smile and walked toward them, just like she had practiced at home. She introduced herself and casually joined their conversation. She mimicked their mannerisms, laughed when they did, and pretended interest in their conversation.

Soon, she felt the same uneasiness as before and excused herself to go to the restroom. The uneasiness, Shawna knew, was God helping her see what she was doing.

"Father, please forgive me for trying to impress others so they'll like me and accept me. Thank You for loving me just as I am. You are sincere, therefore I must be sincere in what I say and do."

With a genuine smile on her face and a spring in her step, she returned with the satisfaction of knowing that she could be herself.

We don't have to work to impress God. He knows who we are, and accepts us with unconditional love.

Lord, help me to sincerely do my best without trying to impress others. Amen.

Children are a gift from the Lord; they are a reward from him.
PSALM 127:3 NLT

Children are our most valuable natural resource.

GOD'S PRECIOUS GIFT

LEIGH TRIED TO KEEP HER EYES ON THE ROAD WHILE HER MIND KEPT REPLAYING DR. KEYES' WORDS LIKE AN OLD SCRATCHED RECORD.

"Congratulations, Leigh! You and Joel are going to have a bonus Christmas present, it seems."

Pregnant? No way! We weren't going to have a baby for three more years. We've booked a cruise in six months. Both our job promotions require travel. We're not ready! she screamed inside her head.

"What is Joel going to say? Will he blame me? We both have been very careful with our birth control. How could this have happened?" she asked as the queasy feeling returned. She had just returned from the bathroom when her husband walked in.

"Honey, are you okay? What did Dr. Keyes find out?" Joel looked worried when he saw his wife's pale face.

"Well, he said we're going to have a special Christmas bonus. But, this one is going to cost us money instead of pay us money." She would have laughed at her husband's sweet, confused face if the situation weren't so serious. After the initial shock, he comforted his tearful wife, assuring her that they probably weren't the only young couple this had happened to.

For days, Joel walked around in a daze while Leigh tried to muster up motherly feelings. She looked at baby clothes and baby furniture. She tried to plan the nursery. But, they only reminded her of the disappointing changes they would have to make. The nausea and tiredness made matters worse.

One day as she waited to see the doctor, another expectant mother sat rubbing her own swollen abdomen. Leigh saw a look of wonder on her face that turned into an angelic smile.

"This is our fourth one, but it always thrills me when I feel my baby move for the first time," she explained. "Words can't describe the awesome feeling of knowing you are giving life to another human being."

My gift to you was My Son, Leigh heard God say in her heart. *And now, you are giving life to another, who is also a gift to you.*

At that moment, Leigh felt a small flutter. She gently rubbed her abdomen in awe. "Lord, thank You for the gift of Your Son and for this precious gift that we're bringing into the world," she whispered, as tears ran down her cheeks.

No matter the size or the wrapping, the gift of a child is priceless.

Lord, I receive my child as a precious gift from You. Please help me to treat him or her with the greatest of love and care. Amen.

Don't be afraid, for I am with you. Do not be dismayed, for I am your
God.   I will strengthen you. I will help you. I will uphold you
with my victorious right hand.
ISAIAH 41:10 NLT

The only thing we have to fear is fear itself.

FAITH IN— FEAR OUT!

NATALIE HAD FELT ILL FOR WEEKS. She couldn't figure out why because she practiced good habits of eating and exercising.

"I don't mean to scare you, but what you described to me sounds like cancer," commented her dearest friend, Joan.

Natalie took a sip of coffee and calmly sat her cup down, even though her insides felt like they were shaking.

"What makes you say that?" she asked, not really wanting to know why.

"Well, I've been reading books about cancer. I figure it's good to be informed. Anyway, you said that you felt . . ."

She's right, Natalie thought as Joan described details and symptoms. *That's how I've been feeling.* Fear clutched at her heart.

"Joan, may I borrow one of the books you've been reading?" she asked, against her better judgment.

Natalie began to read constantly. She couldn't seem to put the book down. Every time she read something, it was like she felt it in her body.

Fear became so intense that she called for an appointment with her doctor for the following week. As soon as she hung up, she picked up the book again.

As she flipped through the pages, Natalie could feel God reach out to her. She felt an urge to put down the book and pick up her Bible.

Once it was open, Natalie quickly turned to a scripture she used to read a lot.

"Don't be afraid; just believe." (LUKE 8:50 NIV) *Do you remember that I told you in My Word not to fear?* an inner voice reminded her. *Fear is not faith. Read My Word to increase your faith.*

"Lord, please help me keep my mind on Your Word," she prayed.

After a thorough exam, Natalie sat across from Dr. Childress as he wrote information on her medical chart. "Well, is it cancer?" she asked, nervously. She hurried on while Dr. Childress looked rather surprised. "I've been reading a lot about it lately. I seem to have all the symptoms."

"Natalie," his gentle voice said, as he took her hand, "you're pregnant. You don't have cancer."

"Dear Lord," she cried with relief and joy. "Forgive me for being afraid."

Both fear and faith grow like plants, but fear is a troublesome weed while faith is a lovely flower. Faith grows best in God's presence.

Lord, help me remember that Your Word strengthens my faith. My faith is simply my belief and trust in You. My belief and trust in You drives out fear. Amen.

Faith, if it does not have works (deeds and actions of obedience to back it up), by itself is destitute of power (inoperative, dead).
JAMES 2:17 AMP

Even if you're on the right track, you'll get run over if you just sit there.

DO SOMETHING!

COLTON FINISHED HIS PRAYERS AND CLIMBED INTO BED. *Tomorrow is it!* he thought. *I graduate with a degree in accounting.* "Lord, I couldn't have done it without You. Some thought I was crazy to go back to college at 45 years old. Some waited for me to fail, but we proved them wrong, didn't we?" he laughed.

After the graduation ceremony, Arthur, a dear friend he hadn't seen in years, rushed over to congratulate him. "What are you doing here?" Colton asked after they finished giving each other a bear hug.

"I flew in for my boss' daughter's graduation. I see there's no need to ask you what you've been doing. I think it's great!" The two friends reminisced for a few minutes and agreed to have lunch the next day.

"How did you manage a family, a full-time job, and school too?" Arthur asked, while they waited for their food.

"It wasn't easy, but I had God's help and my family's prayers. Now, I'm just waiting for God to give me the right job," Colton said.

"If you're interested, there's a position open in the payroll department where I work. Maybe you could take a day off and fly up there,"

Arthur suggested.

"Thanks, but I've prayed and I believe that whatever God wants me to have, He will give it to me," he said with a confident smile. They finished lunch and promised to stay in touch.

Every day, Colton prayed for God to send him a new job. "Lord, I'm waiting on You," he declared day after day.

The days turned into weeks and Colton became discouraged. "Helen," he said to his wife, "I don't understand why I haven't been offered a job. I've been praying and waiting, but nothing has happened."

Helen thought for a moment. "Honey, do you remember telling me on our wedding day that you were sure the first day we met that I was going to be your wife?" she asked.

"Of course I do, but what does that have to do with anything?"

"Well, not only did you tell me that, but you did things to prove it while we dated. Every day you tell me you love me, and you do things to prove it," she said.

Colton slowly began to understand what Helen meant. "Lord, forgive me for being prideful and presumptuous," he prayed. "You helped me finish college. Now, please show me what to do to get the right job." Suddenly, he remembered Arthur's invitation.

"Hello, Arthur. Is that accounting job still available? Good. I'm coming up to apply for it."

If you talk it up, but don't back it up, then you're not on the up and up. Pay closer attention when those around you are speaking. Their message could be the very word from God that you have been looking for.

Lord, please help me be sure to do works of faith that correspond with my words of faith. Amen.

Let us not lose heart and grow weary and faint in acting nobly and doing right, for in due time and at the appointed season we shall reap, if we do not loosen and relax our courage and faint.
GALATIANS 6:9 AMP

I am in earnest—I will not equivocate—I will not excuse—I will not retreat a single inch AND I WILL BE HEARD.

KEEP ON KEEPING ON!

"TRACEY, YOU MUST LOSE 100 POUNDS!" DR. RICHARDS INSISTED. "YOUR LIFE IS AT STAKE," HE WARNED.

"I know, Dr. Richards, but it's hard trying to . . ."

Dr. Richards held up his hand to interrupt Tracey. "I never said anything about an easy way. If it were easy, everyone in America would be slim and trim. What I'm telling you is your body can't continue to handle this pressure," he emphasized.

His voice softened when he saw her eyes well with tears. "My staff and I are here to help you."

"I believe you, Dr. Richards," she said as she wiped her eyes.

Dr. Richards thought for a moment. "Tell you what, let's imagine that you're going on a cruise around the world in your personal yacht. And while you're gone, you decide to have your home remodeled."

Tracey stopped sniffing and looked at him.

"My staff and I are your captain and crew, always at your service to make it smooth sailing," he joked. "The itinerary is for a year. Each port introduces you to a different culture. You disembark to leisurely tour and shop. You buy exquisite furniture, accents and accessories for your home."

Tracey was already daydreaming.

"Now, let's apply all that to your health." Dr. Richards laughed when Tracey' reverie was replaced with confusion. "Each port represents new healthy choices. The furniture, accents, and accessories you buy to beautify your home and make it a joy to live in are the new healthy habits. Now, guess what your home really is," he teased.

Tracey frowned. "I have no idea," she confessed.

He laughed again. "Your home is your body that will be 'remodeled' to be healthy and attractive when you return." Dr. Richards was pleased when Tracey left eager to begin her "cruise".

"Lord, I need strength and patience to finish this," she prayed. She sensed His comforting presence.

Tracey marked off each week on a calendar. Sometimes, the sea became stormy and she stayed longer at port than planned. However, Dr. Richards reminded her that she was gradually establishing a healthy lifestyle. And, just like she gradually gained weight, she would gradually lose it—permanently.

With God's help and Dr. Richards's guidance, Tracey finished her "cruise". After a year, she returned to a "home" filled with health and beauty.

Sometimes a late finish is better than an early start. When you walk the path with God, you can be assured the end will be successful and right on His timetable.

Lord, You were patient as You created this beautiful world. You are patient with me. Please help me to be the same with others and myself. Amen.

My God will liberally supply (fill to the full) your every need
according to His riches in glory in Christ Jesus.
PHILIPPIANS 4:19 AMP

**If you don't have a need, then your greatest need is to help
someone else with theirs.**

TAKEN CARE OF

PATTY LOOKED AT THE MEAGER FOOD IN HER REFRIGER-
ATOR AND PANTRY FOR THE HUNDREDTH TIME AND
SIGHED. She was about to use the last of the bread, peanut butter, and
grape jelly to make sandwiches for her children.

She was a single mom and had recently been laid off. Not only was
it hard because she didn't have enough money, but her car had been
repossessed and she was behind on her house payments.

Just then, she heard Paul and Annie come in the front door. They
thought they were whispering, but their excited voices came through
clearly.

"Our Mommy won't mind feeding you," eight-year-old Paul said.

"Yeah, she won't let you stay hungry," Annie, his little sister agreed.

They walked into the kitchen, holding hands with a new friend.

"Mommy, this is Bobby. He rides the bus with us," Paul said, proudly introducing their friend.

"He just moved here. He's hungry," Annie said.

Patty swallowed her concern and smiled. "I'm very glad to meet you,
Bobby. I hope you like peanut butter and jelly sandwiches." She sent

them to wash their hands while she fixed another place at the table.

"Lord, I have just enough for my children and You send another mouth to feed?" But, she knew, just like her children did, that she couldn't send anyone away hungry. "I'm trusting You to take care of us just like You've done many times before," she prayed. As usual, Patty felt the comfort of God's presence.

While she sat with the children and enjoyed their laughter and chatter, she noticed the expensive clothes and shoes Bobby wore. *Why would he be hungry?* she wondered.

The next morning, after Paul and Annie left for school, Patty heard a knock at her door. When she opened it, a friendly woman smiled and introduced herself.

"I'm Sarah, Bobby's mother. You must be Patty, the one who stole my Bobby's heart with your famous peanut butter and jelly sandwich," she laughed.

Patty laughed too and invited her in for coffee.

Sarah's husband owned a chain of children's clothing stores. They had recently moved to the area because the climate was better for Bobby's allergies. Sarah also confided that they wanted Bobby to have friends who were not influenced by his wealth.

As Sarah got up to leave, she said, "Patty, we really need a computer systems analyst for our district office here. Would you be interested?"

"I sure am," Patty said. *Thank You, Lord!* she thought.

Never think your need is so small that God won't handle it, nor so big that He can't handle it. He's always ready to lend His helping hand.

Lord, I pray that whether my need is small or great, my faith will be constant in Your bountiful provision. Amen.

*Don't repay evil for evil. Don't retaliate when people say unkind
things about you. Instead, pay them back with a blessing. That is what
God wants you to do, and he will bless you for it.*
1 PETER 3:9 NLT

God keeps a better scorecard than you.

PAYBACK

JANICE HURRIEDLY PULLED INTO THE PARKING SPACE.
Suddenly she heard screeching brakes and a honking horn. Startled, she
looked up to see another car jerking to a halt.

"Oh my! I didn't see that car coming. Lord, thank You for protect-
ing both of us," she prayed.

"I'm so sorry," she mouthed to the driver who was swearing at her.
Janice hurriedly backed away from the space and found another one.

She looked at her watch.

"I have one hour to shop before I go to the luncheon," she fussed at
herself. She rushed through the doors, grabbed a shopping cart, and
darted to the bakery. After she picked up some brownies, she quickly
maneuvered her cart to the closest aisle. She was so busy looking at her
list that she wasn't aware of the cart coming in the opposite direction.

"Hey! Look out, stupid!" the angry voice yelled.

Janice looked up to see the driver she had almost hit in the parking
lot.

Oh, not again! she thought.

"What's the matter with you? This is the second time you've tried to kill me!" the woman shouted.

Janice felt anger begin to rise. *After all, I didn't mean to harm her and I could have been hurt too. I apologized and let her have the space. What else can I do?*

Just as she was about to give the woman a piece of her mind, she felt something stop her.

What good would it do? she reasoned. *I'd be upset and late for the luncheon. And she looks like she needs a friend anyway.*

"I was wrong for not paying attention. Please forgive me," Janice offered with a genuine smile.

"My name is Janice. What's yours?" she asked, as the woman stood speechless.

Stop, look, and listen to what God is saying. Usually, you'll find that what you were about to say is very different from the kind words He had planned for you. Allow Him to speak for you. He brings peace in difficult situations.

Lord, please help me to take time to stop and think so that I don't say or do anything wrong to get even with anyone. I want to bless others and be blessed. Amen.

They loved the approval and the praise and the glory that come from men [instead of and] more than the glory that comes from God. [They valued their credit with men more than their credit with God.]
JOHN 12:43 AMP

Compromise is never anything but an ignoble truce between the duty of a man and the terror of a coward.

GET OFF THE FENCE

"MONICA, I HAVE NO CHOICE!" DAVID REMINDED HIS WIFE.

"But sweetheart, you're a Christian. You have no business agreeing to such a thing," Monica said.

"I know I'm a Christian. I also know that I have a family to take care of. Mr. Jones just wants the guys in the office to throw a bachelor party for his son. I already agreed to plan everything, so I can't back out now. What would they all say?"

"Did you know what Mr. Jones expected you to have at this party when he asked you?"

"No, I didn't know. I guess I should have known because of the kind of person his son is. Like father, like son. Monica, you know the kind of person I am. I don't like that kind of entertainment, but they do. I'll do what they both want and I won't go. It's that simple."

"Yes, it is simple. This whole thing is simply wrong, David. And because you know this and you still agree to plan it, you're worse than the ones who come," Monica insisted.

"Mr. Jones is my boss and Josh is his son, and like it or not, I've got to please both of them if I want to keep my job," he said, sheepishly. But David knew his arguments were without merit.

Monica looked David straight in his eyes. "But what about keeping your respect for God? For yourself? For our family? As a Christian, you are a son of God. And likewise, you have a son," she said, firmly. "You said it yourself—like father, like son. I pray for all our sakes you remember that. Good night." She kissed him and went to bed.

"Lord, You know my heart. I don't really want to have anything to do with any of it, but what can I do?" David prayed.

David struggled to go to sleep, but the heaviness in his heart prevented it. He knew what he had to do.

As soon as he arrived at work the next day, he went to Mr. Jones office.

"Mr. Jones, I should never have agreed to plan the bachelor party for Josh. In fact, if I'd known what you both wanted at the party, I would not have agreed to help. It's against my Christian beliefs. I must also provide a godly example for my son. I trust you understand."

When you take a stand on God's word, compromise is not an option. Ask God to show you when to say yes and when to say no.

Lord, in this life there are many opportunities to cross the line or get out of line. But, I prefer to walk the line that You've drawn for me. Amen.

He will remove all of their sorrows,
and there will be no more death or sorrow or crying or pain.
REVELATION 21:4 NLT

The sorrow for the dead is the only sorrow from which
we refuse to be divorced. Every other wound we seek to heal,
every other affliction to forget; but this wound we consider it a
duty to keep open; this affliction we cherish and brood over in
solitude.

THERE IS A TOMORROW

SIX MONTHS HAD PASSED, AND SCOTT STILL SEEMED TO
FEEL HER WARMTH BESIDE HIM.

Melissa, why? he agonized. *Why didn't you tell me that Dr. Jones
warned you not to get pregnant? We could have adopted children. There are
lots of children waiting for parents like us.*

But, there was no more us. His dear sweet Melissa was gone and so
was the dear baby son he would never know. Scott sobbed into his pillow again, just like he did every night.

Scott and Melissa had been married a year when they decided to
begin their family. They both came from large families and could hardly wait to start their own. They had mock arguments about how many
children they wanted.

Scott was a basketball fan and Melissa enjoyed ballet. They often envisioned the sons on the basketball court, and the girls dressed in tutus and performing pirouettes.

But, now the dreams and laughter were gone—forever.

"Lord, what do I have to look forward to?" he cried before he finally drifted into restless sleep.

The next day at work, he saw an ad on the break room bulletin board. It had information about becoming a coach for a junior basketball league. He felt a gentle stirring in his heart.

On Saturday, he went to the community center to meet with the coaching staff. After the meeting, the coaches met with the children and their parents. Scott was immediately surrounded with smiling faces that bombarded him with questions. Small hands slipped into his while others grabbed his pant legs. Scott found himself laughing, returning hugs, and giving handshakes.

That night, Scott's heart was less heavy with grief and sorrow. He finally had a sense of hope. Tomorrow he would begin helping the children in the basketball league. That and the hope of a heavenly tomorrow with Melissa and their son would carry him through.

The loss of a loved one causes grief and sorrow. But, the promise of God's closeness brings hope of a joyful tomorrow.

Lord, I believe You understand the pain of grief and sorrow. Thank You for Your compassionate love that gives me hope that joy will return. Amen.

Love covers a multitude of sins [forgives and disregards the offenses of others].
1 PETER 4:8 AMP

We must evolve for all human conflict a method which rejects revenge, aggression, and retaliation. The foundation of such a method is love.

COVER IT UP!

LEAH WAS TROUBLED BY THE CONVERSATION SHE HEARD WHILE SHE WAITED TO PAY FOR HER GROCERIES. The three ladies directly behind her were whispering how disgusted they were with the new cashier.

Each had a different complaint. Dropped eggs. Mashed bread. Dropped change that scattered on the floor. Failure to scan coupons. Overlooked groceries on the bottom of the cart.

The ladies got louder as other customers began to snicker. They had a captive audience. Some strained to see whom they were talking about. Those who knew rudely pointed at the cashier. There were some who moved to another checkout lane.

Leah was the next in line. She knew if she heard what was going on, the cashier heard it too. The young girl's red face and shaking hands confirmed it.

Leah felt such compassion for her because she remembered her first job as a waitress in the city's only five-star restaurant. She was inexperienced and had not been adequately trained because she was needed immediately. She never forgot the kind gentleman who smiled and offered his handkerchief when she burst into tears after she dropped his plate.

Leah sensed she needed to encourage the girl, but how?

"Hello ma'am," the cashier said with a trembling voice. "Did you find everything satisfactory?"

Leah saw courage and determination in the way she held her shoulders straight and her head erect.

"Everything is just fine, thank you," Leah replied with a smile.

The cashier was very attentive and as accurate as she was fast. Leah had not seen anyone so skillful. She couldn't possibly be the same person those ladies complained about.

The store manager walked by just as the cashier was bagging Leah's groceries.

"This young lady is great," Leah said to him. She spoke loud enough for the women to hear. "You had better hold onto her. I own the shop next door and I could use someone like her on my staff."

Leah winked at the grateful cashier while the ladies in line looked at her with shock.

God's love covers your shortcomings. Allow your love for Him to cover the faults of others.

Lord, when I'm tempted to talk about others' shortcomings, please help me remember how Your love covered mine. Amen.

Finally, brothers, whatever is true, whatever is noble, whatever is right, whatever is pure, whatever is lovely, whatever is admirable—if anything is excellent or praiseworthy—think about such things.

PHILIPPIANS 4:8 NIV

Human thought is the process by which human ends are ultimately answered.

WHAT ARE YOU THINKING?

ALTHEA COULDN'T HELP THINKING ABOUT HOW CRITI-CAL MRS. HOLLAND WAS OF HER. *I know she's Reverend Holland's wife, but does she have the right to say anything she pleases?*

It all began the Sunday Rev. Holland had asked Althea to consider becoming the church's minister of music. He asked her to pray and give him an answer before he met with the choir and musicians the following month. Gina, the current minister of music, was planning to leave in two months because of her husband's new job.

Althea had been a member of the choir for five years and was thrilled to be offered the leadership role. But, no matter how much she wanted the job, she wanted to be sure she was in the will of God. She sensed God was pleased, so she told Rev. Holland she would be honored to do it.

The meeting was twofold. They were saying a fond farewell to Gina and welcoming Althea as their new minister of music.

Rev. Holland presented Gina with a gift from the church and thanked her for her years of service. After the standing ovation, Gina asked Althea to come forward. She and Rev. Holland spoke about

Althea's zeal, dedication, and sacrifice. They talked about her love for God and people. They talked about how her beautiful voice moved people to tears and led them to cry out to God. Then, Rev. Holland announced Althea as their new minister of music.

During the thunderous applause, Althea noticed that Mrs. Holland sat primly and hardly clapped. While refreshments were being served, Mrs. Holland pulled Althea aside. "Althea, my dear, Rev. Holland and I don't always see eye to eye. But, he is the pastor, and as such, his is the last word when it comes to church matters. However, from one woman to another, I believe that I can help you look better so that you present yourself well in your new role."

Althea stood rooted to the floor as Mrs. Holland pointed out everything she considered improper about Althea–from her hair and makeup to her clothes, and even the way she walked. She didn't notice Althea's complete silence.

"I tried to help Gina too, but she didn't listen," Mrs. Holland said, as she shook her head and walked away.

On the way home Althea rehearsed all the hurtful things Mrs. Holland said about her. She tried to think about other things, but she could still hear Mrs. Holland's voice.

"Help Lord," she prayed.

Suddenly, she seemed to hear Gina and Rev. Holland. "Love for God and people. Beautiful voice. Dedicated. Zealous."

"Thank You, Lord. I choose to keep my mind on these good things. And on what I know You want me to do."

Eventually, whatever is at the back of your mind will come to the front. And, whatever you let into your mind will be on your mind. Choose to think on good things.

Lord, please help me keep my mind on You. Then, I know that whatever I think will be good and true. Amen.

"No man will be able to stand before you all the days of your life. Just as I have been with Moses, I will be with you; I will not fail you or forsake you."
JOSHUA 1:5 NASB

I have ever deemed it more honorable and more profitable, too, to set a good example than to follow a bad one.

FOLLOW ME!

THOMAS LOOKED AT SHARON AS SHE HELD THEIR NEW-BORN SON. "Lord, You have entrusted us with this precious life. We have the great responsibility to train Kevin to follow You just as we do. We ask for Your help as we dedicate him to You," Thomas prayed.

Thomas and Sharon were missionaries, and had been married eight years before Kevin was born. Their church relocated them to a different country every two years.

They learned the native language so they could effectively communicate with the people. They worked, ate, and slept with them. They celebrated the births of their children and grieved with them when loved ones died. They learned their culture and taught them some American culture. They taught them God's Word and made themselves available to pray any time. They loved the people and the people loved them.

When Kevin was five years old, Thomas and Sharon returned to the mission field. Kevin was taught to love and serve others just like his parents did. Whatever country they were in, Kevin quickly learned to pray and teach God's Word in that native tongue.

Often Sharon watched Kevin mimic Thomas when he prayed or read his Bible. Sharon remembered Thomas' prayer the day Kevin was born.

The years passed quickly, and Kevin matured into a wonderful young man who inherited his father's love for missions. When his father and mother needed well-deserved rest, Kevin took over every duty, and he did it with joy.

Shortly after he turned 20 years old, Kevin met a young lady with the same passion to love and serve others. They were married and the following year their first son was born.

Thomas and Sharon cried as they watched Kevin pray for his newborn son and dedicate him to God, just as they had done more than 21 years ago. The Lord had helped them to train Kevin, in word and deed, to become a faithful follower of Christ. God's presence was with them and would also be with Kevin and his family.

Our lives are made of words and deeds. We must train our children to follow Christ just as we do—in word and deed.

Lord, You are Truth. You never say one thing and do another. I pray to live the same way before my children. Amen.

[Confine yourself to your own wife] . . . be blessed [with the rewards of fidelity], and rejoice in the wife of your youth. Why should you, my son, be infatuated with a loose woman, embrace the bosom of an outsider, and go astray?
PROVERBS 5:17-18, 20 AMP

The secret of a good life is to have the right loyalties and to hold them in the right scale of values.

HOLD ONTO YOUR OWN!

DAVID WATCHED LYDIA WALK PAST HIS DESK. *Her hair. Her mouth. Her legs,* he thought. He lowered his head in shame and blushed. *You idiot,* he fussed at himself. *You are fifty-five, and a married man with children and grandchildren.* He sighed and returned to his task.

Late that night, David drove into his garage and just sat. He felt old and tired. He picked up his briefcase and went through the garage to the kitchen. His supper was in the microwave, but he wasn't hungry. He trudged upstairs. Each step felt like quicksand.

JoAnn, his wife, was asleep. He quietly put on his pajamas and got in bed. *I thought midlife crisis was over.* Yet he knew he was just looking for excuses. He fell asleep with Lydia on his mind.

The next day their supervisor assigned Lydia and David to a large business tax account. He needed it in two months, and it would require long hours. David and Lydia agreed to discuss the account over dinner.

David stammered as he explained everything to JoAnn over the phone. "I'll be working late for the next two months."

"Okay, honey. I'll miss you. I love you."

"I love you too." The guilt almost choked him.

Lydia's presence intoxicated him. At first they merely discussed the account, but each week their conversation became more personal. They realized their relationship was becoming more than just business. They finished the account on schedule. At their last dinner, they decided to continue seeing each other. He planned to move in with Lydia and ask JoAnn for a divorce. On the way home David argued against the conviction in his heart.

I feel more alive than I have in years! he reasoned. *I can't go back to my old life!* But his heart convicted him.

Is a few moments of pleasure really worth giving up a relationship you know I have created for you?

David knew that voice. It was God warning him not to carry the relationship any further. For the next few moments, he sat alone in the car and cried.

When he went inside, David saw candelabras on the table. Romantic music was playing. JoAnn looked lovely in a new gown. She took him by the hand and they danced. Then they sat down to his favorite meal. They laughed and talked for hours.

JoAnn fell asleep in David's arms. He knew he would never have this comfort, peace, and joy with Lydia.

"Lord, forgive me for being unfaithful to You and JoAnn." Tears ran down his face. "Please show me how to keep our love alive. And help me ask for JoAnna and Lydia's forgiveness."

He fell asleep planning a romantic getaway with his wife.

If your marriage feels old, God can teach you how to renew it. Ask Him for His suggestions.

Lord, You ordained marriage. Please help us honor You and each other and keep our marriage exciting and satisfying so we never tire of each other. Amen.

*I strive always to keep my conscience clear
before God and man.*
ACTS 24:16 NIV

Keep conscience clear, then never fear.

A CLEAR
CONSCIENCE

IT WAS A WEEK BEFORE CHRISTMAS. Mike and Dan watched as their sons, Mark and Clayton, rushed to the electronics store in the mall to look for the Nintendo GameCube system. They didn't know their fathers had already bought them each a game system for Christmas.

Two days before Christmas, Dan had to leave town on unexpected business. He would return late on Christmas Eve, so he asked Mike to wrap Clayton's system and keep it in his attic along with Mark's. Dan would come and get it as soon as he returned.

While descending the ladder from the attic after retrieving Clayton's system, Mike slipped. He thought he heard something crack as the box struck the floor.

Even the Styrofoam packaging couldn't prevent damage from that high up, Mike thought.

Opening the package, Mike's fears were confirmed. The casing on the system was cracked. What was he to do? The stores had closed early, so there was no way to replace it. Maybe he could wrap it anyway and pretend nothing had happened. Despite feeling guilty, Mike followed through with his plan.

While his family slept, Mike waited up for Dan. He tried watching television, but for some reason he could not find any joy in the Christmas favorites he usually watched. Everywhere he turned, the shows talked about peace. Peace on earth. Peace with your fellow man. Peace within yourself.

Mike didn't have peace because of his guilty conscience. "Lord, my son has wanted this Game Cube for a long time. It would be so easy for me to pretend I know nothing about what happened, but You and I know. My conscience won't let me do that. I'll just give him Mark's and pray that Mark will understand." Then, he felt the comforting peace of God in his heart.

When Mike opened the door, Dan offered him a wrapped package. He reminded Mike that both boys preferred the silver Game Cube. The ones they had bought earlier were black. So, Dan had decided to buy the silver ones and he and Mike would return the black ones.

Mike gave him a hug and began to explain what had happened.

When you have a clear conscience, you can make wise decisions. Peace will be the result regardless of the circumstances.

Lord, help me keep a good clear conscience so that no matter what, I have peace within. Amen.

If he had taken warning, he would have saved himself.
EZEKIEL 33:5 NIV

"Look out! and "Be careful!" might be two of the greatest defensive
weapons.

FOREWARNED IS FOREARMED

LAURA LOOKED AT THE MEDICAL ALERT BRACELET
AROUND HER WRIST. Diabetes was engraved on it, along with her
current medicines and those she was allergic to. It was a constant
reminder of the disease that threatened her life. She felt such resentment
that she snatched it off and threw it on the floor.

"I'm doomed to a life sentence of cannots and do nots, she said
aloud. She sat on her bed and cried bitterly.

Dr. West had given her written instructions, and then he warned her
about the consequences of eating and drinking the wrong things. He
told her how to look for certain symptoms, what they meant, and what
to do if they occurred. Her prescriptions also came with warnings.

"Laura, these guidelines are not your enemies," the doctor had told
her. "They alert you to know what to do or not do. Then, diabetes can't
get the best of you. As you follow instructions and heed the warnings,
you can avoid the serious problems that might arise later."

Laura calmed herself as she remembered what Dr. West had said.
Then, she remembered what she had read in the Bible the other day.

God had given the Israelites specific instructions and warned them not to disobey. He did it so they would not encounter trouble.

Laura put the bracelet back on. She thanked God for her life. Her bracelet was a strong reminder for her to follow instructions—her doctor's and God's.

Do you become resentful or feel angry when someone gives you a warning? Turn those negative feelings and thoughts around. Thank God that He loves you enough to alert you to trouble or danger so you can avoid it.

Lord, thank You for the warnings You give me. I know this is one way You prove Your love for me and Your concern for my welfare. Amen.

Give respect and honor to all to whom it is due.
ROMANS 13:7 NLT

Any person of honor chooses rather to lose his honor
than to lose his conscience.

HONOR GOD
AND MAN

THOMAS HUNG UP THE PHONE AND LOOKED AT THE
CLOCK ON THE WALL. *I've only got a couple of hours to get four more
contracts for Mr. Washington,* he thought. *Lord, please help me.*

Thomas had worked six years for the insurance agency and was the
top producer. Mr. Washington had taken him under his wing when he
was fresh out of college and taught him everything he knew. Thomas
looked up to him as his mentor. Not only was Mr. Washington wise and
successful, but he was also an honorable man who respected others.

"Tom, I don't blame a man for what he doesn't have, because I've
been there too," Mr. Washington had told Thomas the day he was hired.
"But, I do blame a man for lying."

Thomas made another call. "Hello, my name is Thomas . . . ."

Yes, another one! He smiled. He made another call and another—all
with success. He looked at the clock again. Only 45 minutes left to get
the last contract. He felt confident.

"Please give me a call if you change your mind," he said, trying not
to sound disappointed. Thomas looked desperately at the clock.

"Lord, I don't want this for myself. I want this for Mr. Washington. He's done so much for me. This is my way to honor him and show him my appreciation for all he's done for me," he prayed softly.

Thomas made the last call. "Yes, thank you very much . . ." he said, pleased to have another client. "Thank You, Lord."

That evening, in Bible study, Mrs. Rothman taught from John 5:23 about honoring God and His Son, Jesus Christ.

Thomas remembered when he had asked God to help him get the contracts for Mr. Washington. "Lord, thank You for putting Mr. Washington in my life. But, dear Lord," he humbly prayed, "my words can barely express my thankfulness for all You have done for me and how much I desire to please You. From the depths of my heart I love You and honor You above all."

It may seem easier to honor those people in your life here on earth. But your Heavenly Father's presence should be just as real. Remember to honor Him above all others.

Lord, I know there are people I must honor, whether they deserve it or not. You are more than deserving of my highest honor. I pray I never forget that. Amen.

He...prayed saying, My Father . . . not what I will [not what I desire],
but as You will and desire.
MATTHEW 26:39 AMP

I'll go where you want me to go, dear Lord,
O'er mountain or plain or sea;
I'll say what you want me to say, dear Lord,
I'll be what you want me to be.

OBEDIENT

YOU ARE EXCITED THAT YOU JOINED THIS WONDERFUL
CHURCH! You look forward to each service. You listen attentively to
the pastor's messages. You worship and praise God along with the congregation. You attend prayer meetings during the week. You gladly give
offerings to help further the Gospel. You meet new friends, grow, and
mature in love and faith as never before. Now, you would like to share
God's love with others.

You pray for His divine direction to show you where to become part
of the church outreach. *Which one, Lord?* you wonder. *Should I deliver
hot meals to the shut-ins? Serve in a soup kitchen? Prepare Thanksgiving
food baskets or buy toys at Christmas?*

His answer disappoints you. Your pastor and his wife approach you
after prayer service. They have a list of members who are sick or shut-in
and need telephone calls of encouragement.

The pastor and his wife see how your cheerful laughter turns someone's frown into a smile, your kind words uplift the discouraged, and

your compassionate prayer ease the grief over the loss of a loved one. They observe your patient understanding soothe hurt feelings.

"Will you please pray and ask the Lord if this is His will for you?" they ask.

This is not what I had in mind. I don't want to do this! You want to protest. But outwardly, you politely smile and say, "I'm honored that you considered me. I will pray about it."

You pray as soon as you return home. "Lord, I know this is not about me or what I desire. This is about pleasing You and blessing others. So, Your will is my will." You sense His peace as you call the pastor to accept your new responsibility.

You call the first name on the list.

"Hello," the weak voice answers.

"Hello, Mrs. Philcott. I'm . . . ."

Mrs. Philcott's voice sounds stronger by the end of your call.

"I'm so glad you called. I appreciate the visit last week, but it's good to have someone to talk to. And, the prayer strengthened me. Call again soon!"

Obedience to God overrules what you want or don't want, and what you like or don't like. God is pleased when you choose to place His desires before yours.

Lord, forgive me for making decisions based on my feelings and my preferences. By Your Spirit, help me say yes to Your will. Amen.

No one claimed that any of his possessions was his own,
but they shared everything they had.
ACTS 4:32 NIV

Sharing lets one know he is important and cared about.

SHARE AND
SHARE ALIKE

ANGIE STEPPED OUT OF HER VAN AND WALKED TO THE
LOBBY. *My traveling companions,* she thought affectionately as she
smiled and waved at the dear ladies she had grown to love. *Norma,
Marilee, Gladys, Susan, Grace, Helen, and Lucille.* She silently listed their
names as she helped them buckle in. They lived within a few doors of
each other in a housing complex for the elderly. All were in their 70s, but
they were a lively bunch. They attended the same church as Angie.

Angie remembered the first time she had given them a ride home
from church two years ago. They stood outside in the drizzle, huddled
under a huge golf umbrella, waiting for the church van to return from
carrying the first passengers. Angie pulled alongside and volunteered to
take them home.

They lived only five minutes from Angie, but they insisted on paying her when she dropped them off. The next Sunday, they had
approached her again and from then on, it became a regular thing.

Angie had become annoyed when they continued to impose like
that. She began to avoid them. Then Reverend Gaines preached about

how the believers in the book of Acts shared everything they had. Their possessions were for everyone to use, so no one was destitute or in need. Angie knew God was speaking to her heart and from that moment, she had a good attitude about giving them a ride.

Her thoughts were interrupted when she felt her van hesitate as she changed gears. Then, it really strained to climb a slight hill. The next day, her mechanic told her the transmission would need to be replaced. All Angie could think about was that she had less than a hundred dollars in her savings account.

Angie prayed that God would provide a way to get her van fixed and for her friends to find a ride to church. Then she called Norma to tell her what the mechanic had said. She apologized for being unable to pick them up next Sunday.

On Saturday, Angie received a call from a car dealership saying that some friends of hers were buying her a new van. The salesman asked what time she'd be able to drop by and pick the one she wanted. He chuckled as he told her the friends had insisted he arrange it today because they had to have a ride to church on Sunday.

God shares everything He has with us. Consider how God's love is displayed when our attitude is, "If I have it, then you also have it." We become givers—like God.

Lord, You shared Your love with me by giving up Your Son for me. I desire to live a selfless life – not a selfish one—so others can know Your love. Amen.

Don't set your heart on anything that is your neighbor's.
EXODUS 20:17 MSG

The Lord rejoices when you rejoice with others in their success.

GET YOUR OWN!

GREG LET OUT A LONG WHISTLE WHEN HE SAW THE SLEEK, BLACK CONVERTIBLE STAN POINTED TO. It was a two-seater with leather interior and all the extras.

They talked with the salesman, grabbed some brochures, and started back to their office. They almost quarreled as each tried to formulate a perfect plan to buy the car.

They had been friends since high school. Greg's parents were wealthy but had raised him to work hard to achieve success. Stan's mother was a hardworking single mom who had taught him the value of thankfulness and truthfulness.

"Don't ever desire what Greg has because it's his. Be glad for him and be thankful for what you have. Think and choose what's right, say and do what's right, and God will give you your own." Stan's mother had encouraged him with those words when Greg got something new that Stan and his mother weren't able to afford.

After high school, they had attended the same university. Greg became a CPA while Stan became a financial advisor. After interning at Greg's father's accounting firm, they established their own business. Their parents were proud of the success of their friendship and their business.

One Saturday morning, a month after they saw the car, Stan heard loud honking outside his townhouse. He looked out his living room window and saw Greg grinning and waving. He sat in the very same convertible they had seen at the car dealership!

Stan raced downstairs, threw open his front door, and stood there with his mouth agape. *Lord, I want that car! That should be my car because I saw it first!* he thought, aggravated with Greg. Old feelings of jealousy surfaced—just as he had experienced as a teen when Greg got something new. Right then, he again heard his mother's voice and remembered her words.

"Mom, you're right. I'm going to get my own some day. God is going to see that I do," he whispered and then he ran to congratulate his friend.

Your Heavenly Father will grant you the desires of your heart. He enjoys blessing you as much as He enjoys blessing others.

Lord, help me rejoice when You bless others. I don't desire what they have because I know You have specific blessings just for me. Amen.

Whatever your hand finds to do, do it with all your might.
ECCLESIASTES 9:10 NIV

Sincere help hears the cry, answers the need, and touches the heart.

HELP OUT!

KATE GREETED EVERYONE WHO CAME INTO THE CHURCH LOBBY WITH A SMILE, A HUG, OR A HANDSHAKE. She was able to remember names and she was a great listener. This helped her as she made visitors feel welcome and chatted briefly with familiar friends.

Still, she was nervous because this was only her second week as a greeter, and she was by herself. *Why would Stella put me here alone knowing I'm new at this?* she wondered.

After the service, several visitors thanked her for her warm welcome. Stella, the hospitality club president, lauded her for a job well done.

What's so special and important about it? Anyone can smile and say hello, she thought. *It's not some great feat and it doesn't require special training.*

As if she heard Kate's thoughts, Stella said, "I know some people think anyone can be a greeter, but they're wrong. Sometimes a smile, hello, and words of greeting aren't sincere, but yours are. You have a God-given talent for encouraging people. Don't take it for granted—I don't."

Kate got up early to pray and read her Bible the next morning. She sensed a need to pray about something having to do with the bank where she worked.

After returning from lunch, the elevator got stuck with she and approximately twenty others in it. She recognized some of her coworkers, but there were several unfamiliar faces and a few children.

Kate felt panic begin to choke her. But, then she saw the terror on the faces and heard it in the voices of the others as they beat on the doors and screamed for help.

"Lord, help me stay calm so I can help these people stay calm," she prayed. The Lord reminded her of what Stella had said.

Kate took a deep breath and put a smile on her face. She made the emergency call for help and then suggested they pray. This helped them relax. Then, she applied the same skills she had used Sunday. She greeted the strangers like she had the visitors and spoke to her co-workers as if they were members. She called each person by name as she talked to them, and encouraged them to talk amongst themselves.

An hour later, the elevator started again. Before they got off, each person hugged her and thanked her for her help.

"Lord, now I know that every skill and talent You put in me is valuable for building others up. Thank You.

No one cares who you are not or what you do not have when trouble or tragedy comes. What matters is that you are present and have a compassionate and willing heart to help.

Lord, show me how to look past my inadequacies when there is a cry for help. Thank You for helping me to answer that cry. Amen.

Give instruction to a wise man, and he will be still wiser;
Teach a just man, and he will increase in learning.
PROVERBS 9:9 NKJV

Keep getting more knowledge and learning more answers because new problems and more questions come every day.

KEEP LEARNING!

SCOTTY TRIED TO ACT LIKE A SOPHISTICATED BUSINESS-MAN. He hoped his excitement wasn't too obvious. He listened as Mr. Graves offered his electrical company the contract for the newest and largest office complex in the city.

He had been an electrician for thirty years, having learned the trade from his father and grandfather. With God's help, he had run one of the city's most successful companies for the last twenty years. His company had a reputation for excellent work and skilled workers.

The day after he signed the contract, Scotty had a meeting with his employees. While they were laughing, slapping each other on the back, and giving each other high-fives, God spoke to Scotty's heart.

You know a lot, but you need to know a lot more.

"Lord, what do You mean? What do You want me to do?" he prayed. The answer God gave him wasn't going to make his employees very happy. But, he knew they trusted him, and he trusted God.

The incredulous looks and open mouths would have been amusing if Scotty hadn't known the seriousness of God's instructions.

"Refresher courses? Boss, you've got to be kidding!" said Jack, a long-time employee and old friend.

"I know this has been a surprise, so the company would like to cover your expenses."

Heads began to nod in agreement.

"It won't be easy, but we can do it if we make the effort and take the time. I'll have my secretary call the community college for information. According to the contract, we have just enough time to complete the classes and the project. And, as all of you know, I don't ask you to do anything I won't do myself. So, I'll see you in class!"

They were still laughing when the meeting ended.

Within a short time, all of them successfully completed the courses. After the ribbon-cutting ceremony, Mr. Graves approached Scotty about plans for a new housing development.

Your Heavenly Father has given you a sound mind (2 Timothy 1:7 KJV) to successfully acquire knowledge and skills. Remember, there's always more to learn, and the best way to learn is to follow God's direction.

Lord, I believe You desire me to not only keep learning the things that pertain to Your kingdom, but the practical things of this world as well. Thank You for helping me to be successful in both areas. Amen.

The sheep listen to his voice. He calls his own sheep by name . . . and his sheep follow him because they know his voice.
JOHN 10:3-4 NIV

There is no knowledge that is not power.

KNOW FOR YOURSELF

JOAN QUICKLY SCANNED THE MENU AS SHE SAT WITH MELISSA AND JUDY, HER NEIGHBORS. They were helping Melissa shop for her baby's nursery and had stopped to eat lunch.

"I'm hungry as a horse," Melissa said. "I think I'm going to order fries with my hamburger today."

Judy laughed. "Yeah, with a baby on the way, you'd better order pie too!"

Suddenly, Melissa got quiet and her friends became concerned.

"Oh, there's nothing wrong," Melissa said with a reassuring smile. "I was just recalling that my doctor said I have to eat right for me and my baby. In fact, he gave me several books to help me learn healthy eating habits. I'm learning about the changes in my body and how my baby is developing."

Melissa stopped talking so they could order their food; then she resumed. "I'm learning what foods are good and bad for me. I'm trying to stay in tune with my body so I see the warning signs when something's wrong. The more I learn, the easier it'll be for me to make healthy choices. The doctor said I'll get a lot of advice, but some will be old wives' tales, and it's up to me to make the right decisions."

That night, Joan lay awake. She remembered what Melissa had said and it made her think about her spiritual life. She had been a Christian for a while and she loved God with all her heart, but she was dissatisfied with her spiritual growth. She often based decisions on other Christians' opinions and followed their advice, even when she didn't feel it was right for her. She was hesitant to make a move on her own because she feared she'd make a mistake. She felt she pleased everyone but God.

"Lord, I've depended on the faith of others. I've made decisions based on what they say. Help me develop the faith to believe I can know Your voice for myself. I realize that as I read Your Word and pray, You will teach me. I know You will lead me to make wise decisions and good choices."

No matter how much you hear from others, what you learn and know for yourself is what matters.

Lord, while I appreciate the counsel of other Christians, my heart's desire is to hear and know Your voice for myself. Amen.

Be joyful always; pray continually; give thanks in all circumstances, for this is God's will for you in Christ Jesus.
1 THESSALONIANS 5:16-18 NIV

No longer forward nor behind I look in hope or fear;
But, grateful, take the good I find,
The best of now and here.

ATTITUDE OF GRATITUDE

SUPPOSE YOU ARE ALREADY LATE FOR WORK AND YOUR CAR HAS A FLAT TIRE. Or the driver in front of you has a right turn signal on, but suddenly decides to turn left. Or perhaps you're at lunch when the saltshaker top comes off and instead of shaking the salt out, you pour it on your food.

How would you handle circumstances such as this? Cry? Throw a tantrum? Punch or kick something? Swear? Grumble, gripe, or complain the whole day?

Unexpected annoyances are part of life. The way we respond to them is what matters most. Your reaction is a good measure of your attitude toward life. You can choose to let such disturbances worry or depress you. Instead, ask the Holy Spirit to help you express thanks for the positive things in your life.

For example, be thankful your tire didn't go flat on the highway.

Give thanks that you didn't run into the car that turned in front of you. While you pray for the people in the accident that caused the stalled traffic, remain thankful that you are alive and well.

An attitude of thankfulness will help you see God's goodness in every situation.

Life is not always predictable, nor is it always pleasant. A thankful attitude will help you overcome and bring you into God's presence frequently.

Lord, I know my attitude plays an important part in my success. By Your Spirit, help me give thanks when things don't go the way I plan. Amen.

*All your sons will be taught by the Lord, and great will
be your children's peace.*
ISAIAH 54:13 NIV

You are the bows from which your children
as living arrows are sent forth.

MY CHILD IS
GOD'S DISCIPLE

ELIZABETH LOOKED AT KYLE, HER FIFTEEN-YEAR-OLD
SON, STANDING IN THE BAGGAGE CLAIM AREA OF THE AIR-
PORT. She hardly recognized him. He was dressed in black, from head
to toe. *Why does he do that?* Elizabeth wondered as she noticed his black
lips, nails, and spiked hair. His ears, eyebrows, and nose were pierced.
He wore an ankle-length coat.

It's 95 degrees outside! she thought. *He was only there a week! How dare
Dale send him home looking like this!* she fumed.

When Elizabeth heard people whispering and saw them pointing at
Kyle, she felt love for her son well up in her heart. *Lord, I want to display the compassion and love You felt for me when I was rebellious. Please
help me be patient with Kyle.*

Kyle had begun visiting his father when Dale and Elizabeth divorced
two years earlier. Elizabeth prayed and released him into God's care
before each visit. Each time, he returned more restless, moody, and dis-
tant. The Lord's presence comforted Elizabeth and helped her become

more patient.

She constantly prayed, "Lord, no matter what, Kyle is my son and Your disciple. I taught him Your Word. He obeys it and has Your peace."

One Sunday morning before church, Kyle was being deliberately stubborn and would not leave his room. Elizabeth waited an hour before he sauntered downstairs. Instead of scolding him, she felt the urge to pray with him. Kyle didn't resist as Elizabeth hugged him and prayed.

"Mom, I'm so sorry," he sobbed. "I get so confused when I visit Dad. It's like he hates God and he disagrees with everything you taught me from the Bible. I love him, but each trip gets worse. I feel at peace when I'm home with you."

When you've taught your children God's Word, don't become discouraged or give up hope when they disobey. God is with them as He is with you.

Lord, I've taught my children Your Word. They remember and obey it. They are filled with Your peace. Amen.

I will be with you; I will not fail you or forsake you.
JOSHUA 1:5 AMP

Being alone does not mean being lonely.

NEVER ALONE!

As Troy drove home from his lawyer's office, he rubbed the slight indentation on his finger where the wedding band used to be. He had developed the habit during the last five years. His ring hadn't been fancy—just a simple, thin gold band that matched Beth's. They had decided to keep life simple.

They had been madly in love and were determined to stay married for life. That was the original plan. However, he had discovered that plans sometimes change.

How could he have known that he was unable to father the children they both desired? Nothing prepared him for her reaction to his decision to become a Christian? She opposed it saying that it put too many limitations on their lives. As he matured in the Lord, their marriage fell apart. Troy turned to God for comfort. He read the book of John and how Jesus' followers deserted Him because they didn't understand the truth He taught.

Meanwhile, Beth had turned to the sympathetic ear of Troy's best friend, who eventually fathered her first child just before the divorce. It had all came to a bitter end today.

Troy pulled into his driveway and looked at the dark, lonely house. No wife, no children—not even a dog to greet him. The loneliness and despair were almost too painful to bear.

"Lord, if I were the only person on this planet, I don't think I could be any more lonely than I am right now," he whispered.

I understand that feeling, the voice said in his heart. *When I was on the Cross, separated from My Father, I felt the same way. I'm right here. I won't leave you.*

"Thank You, Lord," he prayed as tears welled his eyes. "I'm not alone anymore."

Have you ever felt so lonely that you were desperate to talk to or be with someone? Your Heavenly Father is never too busy or too tired. Call to Him. He is a wonderful listener.

Lord, help me remember that I might not always have another human being to talk to or be with. But, I always have You. Amen.

All who listen to me will live in peace and safety, unafraid of harm.
PROVERBS 1:33 NLT

"Safety is from God alone."

SAFE AND SOUND

THE SNOW SWIRLED OUTSIDE AND FORMED A SOFT, GLISTENING BLANKET OVER CASSIE'S LAWN. *It's absolutely beautiful!* she thought. She remembered that each snowflake has a different pattern.

"Heavenly Father, You are truly the magnificent Creator." The weather report said that only a couple of inches would fall before it ended the next morning. However, she made sure she had the necessary emergency provisions in case it got worse.

"Finally, I get to use my new gas fireplace." After she lit it, Carrie settled down with a novel, a blanket, and cup of hot chocolate. She felt uneasy and couldn't focus on her novel.

"What's the matter, Lord? Am I missing something?" she asked.

Bonnie, her Labrador retriever, barked. Carrie sensed she needed to bring her indoors. *But why? She's well protected in her insulated doghouse,* Carrie reasoned. Bonnie barked louder as Carrie brought her into the mudroom.

She returned to her warm fire, but Bonnie howled. "OK, girl, you can share the fireplace with me." Carrie rubbed Bonnie's head as they both fell asleep on the rug.

What's happened? I feel so cold. Carrie struggled to wake up. *Why won't my eyes open? Why can't I get up?*

She seemed to hear Bonnie barking from a long distance. Cassie coughed and tried to take deep breaths. *What's that awful odor? Why is my face cold and wet?*

"Help, Lord!" she cried.

Cassie opened her eyes. Bonnie was licking her face. Cassie heard someone yelling her name and banging on her door. She was dizzy and weak, but she struggled to her feet. Holding onto Bonnie's collar, she stumbled to the door. Several neighbors and some firemen were there.

She found out that an ice storm had blown in. A strong wind caught in the chimney and blew out the flame while she slept. The escaping gas had caused her to fall into a deeper sleep.

Neighbors had heard Bonnie's continuous, loud barking. They looked through Cassie's living room window and saw Bonnie curled up beside her. Bonnie never left Cassie's side, even when they knocked on the window and the door. Someone finally broke a window, smelled the gas and called the fire department.

Cassie thanked God for keeping her safe, and for Bonnie, who like God, never left her alone.

Protection and safety don't always come by man's hands. God can use whatever is available to help us.

Lord, thank You for Your plans for my safety. Help me listen and obey so they protect me. Amen.

Do two walk together unless they have agreed to do so?
AMOS 3:3 NIV

There is no greater partner than the one God chooses for you.

THE RIGHT
PARTNER

LOUIS WAS FIFTEEN YEARS OLD WHEN HE BEGAN TO
DREAM AND PLAN TOWARD OWNING HIS OWN BUSINESS.
Twenty years later he was an accomplished editor working for the city's
main newspaper. He sensed God was preparing him to realize his life-
long dream—starting his own publishing company.

"Lord, we both know I'll need a partner. I ask for Your wisdom and
guidance every step of the way," he prayed.

Later that week, Louis spoke to Benjamin, a close friend, at the men's
fellowship breakfast. Louis wanted to ask Benjamin to be his partner.
After all, who better than someone he had known for ten years? But for
some reason he wasn't comfortable pursuing the topic.

The next day, the managing editor introduced him to Brad, a new
staff writer who was going to work with Louis on a series of stories about
the city's history. Louis was impressed with Brad's skills and enjoyed his
personality. They had much in common and hit it off right away.

Louis prayed constantly about his publishing company. He remembered Psalm 32:8 where God promised to instruct and teach him the

way to go. Several times, he started to ask Benjamin about partnership, but he just couldn't find the right words.

"Lord, I won't force this. You will let me know the right time to ask him."

Louis and Brad began to work long hours together. They won an award for their series of articles. A year later, they won a Pulitzer Prize for the newspaper. As their families celebrated at dinner, Louis felt a nudge to share his dream with Brad. "But, Lord, You know I don't talk about this with anyone except my wife. I haven't even asked Benjamin to . . ." he whispered.

Suddenly, it became clear to him

That's it! he almost yelled at the table. *Lord, You have been showing me my partner for the past eighteen months! This is the right time and Brad is the right person to ask!*

Do you feel confident about the person you desire to be your partner? Whether for marriage, business or pleasure, God will direct you in every relationship if you ask Him for His plan.

Lord, I'm not in such a hurry that I don't take time to ask Your opinion about the person I desire to be my partner. I need Your wisdom and guidance. Amen.

Fire goes out for lack of fuel, and quarrels disappear when gossip stops.
PROVERBS 26:20 NLT

When you don't know what to say, perhaps it's best to pray.

MIND YOUR OWN BUSINESS!

RITA WAS IN HER BACKYARD WATERING HER PRIZE
PETUNIAS. She heard rustling in her neighbor's yard. She wondered if
that pesky squirrel was back that she and Wanda, her neighbor, had seen.
She tiptoed quietly to their adjoining wood fence and peered through a
small knothole.

She glimpsed a woman slipping in the backdoor. Was Wanda back
so soon from grocery shopping? And, where were the groceries? Why
would she be going in the back door? Wanda knew Rita had a key to her
house. They had exchanged spare keys in case of emergencies.

A short time later, Wanda drove into her garage and honked her
horn for Jim to help carry in the groceries. Rita was puzzled when she
heard the horn. Then, she heard whispering and quickly went back to
the fence and looked through the knothole again. The woman was saying goodbye and scurrying through some bushes.

Several times a week for the next month, Rita saw the woman slipping in Wanda's back door. Rita was angry with Jim and couldn't bear to
see Jim treat Wanda as if nothing was going on. The hurt she felt for

Wanda was like what she had felt for her mother, who had gone through the same thing five years ago, after thirty years of marriage.

Rita decided Wanda needed to know what she had seen. After all, the Bible did say to speak the truth to your neighbor (Zechariah 8:16). She prayed that she'd say the right thing. But, when she finished praying, she felt a change of heart.

She remembered her mother's response when friends had thought she ought to confront her husband and the other woman. "Some things are best left alone. They might work it out for themselves." They did after many tears and prayers, and their marriage had been stronger than ever.

"Heavenly Father, forgive me for meddling in Wanda's and Jim's marriage," Rita prayed. "I believe You are capable of handling it. I pray they work things out with Your help."

True concern will encourage you to pray for others to handle their own affairs with God's help. Hear from God and follow His direction.

Lord, forgive me for meddling in anyone's business. Remind me to pray that others would handle their lives responsibly, just as I pray the same for myself. Amen.

The free gift of God is eternal life through Christ Jesus our Lord.
ROMANS 6:23 NLT

The richest gifts we can bestow are the least marketable.

THE GIFT THAT KEEPS ON GIVING

WHAT MAKES THE MANY HANDMADE HOLIDAY GIFTS FROM CHILDREN SO SPECIAL TO THEIR PARENTS? They may have been slightly imperfect, but the recipient sees only the love with which they were given. Often, the flaws make them even more valuable.

Marian considered this as she looked at the Grandparents Day card she had just received from her five-year-old granddaughter, Brianna. Its simply written message of love and the handprint on the inside reminded her of God's special gift to us, His Son, Jesus.

Looking at pictures that depicted Jesus on the cross, Marian could see how He might have appeared "messed up" or "flawed." He had been wounded, whipped, and bruised so badly that he hardly resembled a human. But Marian realized it wasn't His appearance that had the deepest impact on the disciples, or us. It was what His death stood for.

After His Resurrection, Jesus showed the disciples the gaping holes in His hands and side to confirm what He had told them. "Destroy this temple, and in three days I will raise it up," Jesus had said. (John 2:19 KJV)

Glancing at the handprint on the card, Marian pictured Jesus standing before her, His hand outstretched, saying, "This is a symbol of My love for you."

Smiling brightly, Marian realized that just as the flaws in Brianna's picture did not lessen the amount of love she had put into making it, neither did those nail-scarred hands decrease the value of God's gift.

God's gift to man cannot be measured.

There is nothing you can do to earn it or pay for it. You must simply believe Him and receive Him. And when you receive God's Son as a gift, you also receive God's gift of eternal life.

The superficial value of a gift is determined by dollars and cents. The heart determines the true value.

Heavenly Father, I believe You sent Your greatest gift, Your Son, because You loved the world. I receive Your love and Your gift. Amen.

A wise man is mightier than a strong man, and a man of knowledge is more powerful than a strong man.

PROVERBS 24:5 NLT

Success to the strongest, who are always, at last, the wisest and best.

STRENGTH IS MORE THAN MUSCLES

"DAD, COME AND SEE HIM," SCOTT SAID. "He's built like a tank! Don said his dad has been a professional bodybuilder for fifteen years!"

Walter laughed at his thirteen-year-old son's excitement. "Well, I'll just have to meet this new superhero of yours."

"Awesome! And his name is Phil," Scott shouted over his shoulder as he rushed back across the street.

Neighbors had gathered in front of Phil's garage, gawking at the human behemoth. When he finished his squats, bench presses, and lifts, there was thunderous applause.

"Come on, Dad," Scott said, as he grabbed Walter's arm. "I already asked Mr. Phil to help you get in shape. He said he'd be glad to." Walter sucked in his protruding abdomen before he introduced himself to Phil.

Not a day passed that Scott didn't mention some awesome feat of strength Phil performed. "I guess my engineering degree can't compare with Phil's weightlifting titles," Walter grumbled to his wife.

One Saturday morning, Walter knocked on Scott's door to remind him to cut the grass. When there was no answer, he remembered Don had invited Scott over first thing that morning to see his birthday present. Phil had invited Walter to visit also, but Walter didn't want to be pressured into another informal nutrition pep talk and bodybuilding demonstration.

"Lord, forgive me if it's envy, but I just don't want to go," he argued. He began mowing his lawn, but soon quit because he sensed God was urging him to visit Phil.

Why? he wondered as he crossed the street.

"Sweet!" Scott exclaimed when he saw the big box. "A dirt bike!"

"Oh no!" Phil yelled after he opened the box. "I thought it would already be assembled. Where do I begin? I don't even have the tools for this," he moaned, as he looked at the instructions for assembly.

"There's a million pieces in there!" Don said, looking inside.

Walter arrived in time to hear the commotion. He took one quick look and sent Scott for his largest tool kit. He and Scott assembled the bike in record time while Phil and Don watched in amazement.

After many hearty thanks, Walter and Scott left.

"Dad, with all that strength Mr. Phil has, he still couldn't put that bike together. He might have a lot of muscles, but when it comes to brain power, you're my superhero," he grinned

---

Physical health and strength are important, but never underestimate the power of mental soundness. The Bible says in 3 John 2 (NLT), your body should be as healthy as your soul.

Lord, thank You for a sound mind that empowers me to be healthy and strong—physically and in other ways. Amen.

Choose a good reputation over great riches,
for being held in high esteem is better
than having silver or gold.
PROVERBS 22:1 NLT

If I take care of my character, my reputation will take care of me.

YOU
EARNED IT!

MELANIE WAS PLEASED BUT CONFUSED BY THE OFFER HER BOSSES HAD JUST MADE. *Why would they pick me over Rick or Sarah, she wondered. They have both been here much longer than I have.*

Then Melanie remembered her last job evaluation. "You have always been dependable," her manager had told her. "You're self-motivated, you follow through on all your assignments, and you're always on time. We wish others were as diligent as you."

Her father had always encouraged Melanie and her older brother to be diligent in whatever they did.

"Always give an honest day's work for an honest day's pay," he would say.

"Lord, I've always tried to follow that rule," Melanie said under her breath as she walked back to her office. "I realize this is my reward."

In the silence that followed, she could almost hear God answering her. *Yes, it is.* Concern was suddenly replaced with peace. Only God could have orchestrated this new move in her life. Melanie was confident that God would be with her every step of the way.

When you are committed to something, you don't have to convince others. They will know it by your actions.

Thank You, Lord, that I am known by what I do and not what I say I will do. Amen.

Get all the advice and instruction you can,
and be wise the rest of your life.
PROVERBS 19:20 NLT

Most of us ask for advice when we know the answer but
we want a different one.

A WRONG
CHOICE

IT WAS LONELINESS THAT HAD PROMPTED HER TO START
DATING SO SOON AFTER HER HUSBAND'S DEATH, SHE REA-
SONED. Now, the man she was dating wanted to marry her. He was not
a Christian. Lois was finally faced with the truth. Everything in her
wanted to say yes to Arthur's marriage proposal. But she knew it would
be wrong.

Lois decided to pray, thinking, *maybe God will understand and say it's
okay.* But in her heart, she knew that would not happen. Her prayers
were continually interrupted as she remembered the Bible verse that
warned against relationships between Christians and non-believers (II
Corinthians 6:14). Lois knew God was telling her the relationship was
wrong and marriage would certainly be worse.

"Lord, I should never have become involved in this relationship,"
she prayed. "Forgive me for seeking to fill my loneliness with human
companionship. I don't want to hurt Arthur, but I understand that I
am not in Your will."

Lois knew what she had to do. Not only would she tell Arthur no, but she would end the relationship.

There may be times when you make a mistake and find your life going in the wrong direction. But God is always waiting for you to ask for His help. He will lead you back.

Father, I know that as long as I am living I am capable of making a wrong decision. Thank You for helping me recognize when I am off track and for giving me the strength to say no to sin. Amen.

Wounds from a friend are better than many kisses from an enemy.
PROVERBS 27:6 NLT

True friendship is more than just a pat on the back.

FACE IT!

CHARLOTTE READ THE E-MAIL OVER CAREFULLY. She wanted to make sure it conveyed exactly how she felt about Melinda's words. "You hurt me deeply yesterday," the message began. "I don't know if I can ever forgive you."

What followed was a recap of their conversation during lunch the previous day. Charlotte had wanted a true assessment of her job performance since becoming supervisor. She felt Melinda would be honest.

"You're very pushy," Melinda had told her. "And everything has to be done your way or it's wrong." There had been other bits of criticism that Melinda offered. But that had been the worst.

"I thought you were my friend." Charlotte looked at those words in the e-mail message. Then, she thought about the relationship she had with Melinda. Their relationship had always been based on truth and honesty. *She did just what I asked,* Charlotte realized.

Melinda's honesty had been God's way of revealing her mistakes. Chalotte took a moment to think about the last few months. If she took Melinda's words to heart, they could actually help her become a better leader.

Instead of hitting the "Send" button, Charlotte quickly tapped the "Delete" key. Then, she started a new message.

"Hey, girl! Thanks for being honest with me yesterday," she wrote. "You really helped me to see myself in a true light."

When you ask a friend for honesty, are you prepared to receive it? True friends will always speak the truth, regardless of whether it hurts. Ask God to help you to listen and be willing to accept feedback, even when it comes from a friend.

Father, I am thankful that You surround me with friends who love me enough to tell me what I need to hear and not what I want to hear. Amen.

Forgetting the past and looking forward to what lies ahead,
I strain to reach the end of the race and receive the prize for which
God, through Christ Jesus, is calling us up to heaven.
PHILIPPIANS 3:13-14 NLT

Living in the past means you will never walk in the future.

MOVING ON!

TODD AND RACHEL CRIED AS THEY READ THE LETTER. In the year since his discharge from the Air Force, life had been a series of struggles for the two. Their small, furnished apartment was barely large enough for them and their infant daughter. And the 12-year-old car they shared needed repairs.

Todd had not been able to find a steady job since moving to Georgia, and the bills were piling up. The letter carried the weighty news that everything they owned, including their furniture and many sentimental items, was gone. They had been sold at auction when Todd could not pay the storage bill.

"I thought I heard from God when we moved here," Todd told Rachel. The picture he held—showing their young daughter playing with toys last Christmas—was the single reminder of their past. "But now I'm convinced that we missed it."

Thinking back on his quick decision to move from Florida to Georgia, Todd felt convicted. He knew where he had gone wrong. "I didn't pray about this," he told Rachel. "I was so anxious to get away from there that I totally left God out of the picture."

"But it's not too late," Rachel said as she wiped away tears. "We can still pray and ask God for forgiveness and direction."

The two sat quietly for a moment. Then, Todd prayed. As he did, he felt God's arm around his shoulder—holding him tightly. Todd knew God had forgiven him and was about to do something special.

The next day, Rachel received a phone call from Todd's father. He wanted them to move to Virginia and live with him for a while. It would give them time to clear their heads and hear clearly from God.

A month later, Todd accepted a job working as an airplane mechanic at an airport terminal just outside of town. It was the same line of work he had successfully performed while in the military. Rachel took a good-paying position as a medical assistant and began training to receive an associate degree in nursing.

Within a year, the couple moved to their own apartment. They bought new furniture. Their daughter had new toys and loving grandparents nearby.

In church one Sunday, Todd listened carefully as the pastor encouraged the congregation. "Don't live in the past. Press toward the prize God has waiting for you."

"Thank You, Lord, for wiping away our past and giving us a brand new start," Todd prayed softly.

Have you let go of your past so that God can reveal His plan for your life? Don't allow your past to dictate where God can take you in the future.

Lord, thank You for helping me see that I can never prosper by dwelling on past mistakes. Show me the direction You want me to take, and give me strength to go there. Amen.

Search for the Lord and for his strength, and keep on searching.
I CHRONICLES 16:11 NLT

God is not in a box.

CHANGE THE ROUTINE

JULIA SAT QUIETLY AND STARED OUT THE KITCHEN WIN-
DOW. Her husband was at work, the kids were off to school, and she
had finished her chores. Now she could spend some time with God.

But again today, something was wrong. Julia noticed that when she
settled down to read, her thoughts were scattered and she had trouble
concentrating. When she prayed, the words sounded alike. She felt like
she was searching for God and not finding Him.

Lord, what is going on with me? Julia wondered as she flipped through
the pages of her Bible. *All of a sudden everything seems so routine. There's
no excitement!*

Looking across the room, Julia glanced at a picture her three-year-
old had drawn and taped to the refrigerator door. Scrawled above the
images of a tree, a mountain, and some clouds were the words: God
Made All This.

Taking another glance out the kitchen window, Julia thought about
those words. *Instead of waiting for Him to come to me, maybe I should go
to Him,* she thought.

Taking up her Bible, note pad, and pens, Julia walked from the kitchen out onto the patio. The sound of birds singing and the feel of the cool breeze blowing against her skin assured her that God was already there.

"Thank You, Lord, for joining me this morning," she prayed aloud as she opened her Bible.

Just as our daily schedules can become routine and boring, so can the private time we spend with God. Try something different. Go to the park. Take a walk. Get on the treadmill. Then, talk to God. He will meet you wherever you are.

Thank You, Father, that you meet me wherever I am and that my time with you is not routine, but new every morning. Amen.

If a person is ashamed of me and my message, I, the Son of Man, will be ashamed of that person.
LUKE 9:26 NLT

Be more ashamed to do wrong than ashamed to do right.

NO
SHAME

"GLENDA," BILL SAID TO HIS WIFE, "CHESTER ATE LUNCH WITH US TODAY."

Glenda looked concerned. "Isn't Chester the young Christian you've been praying for?" Bill braced himself for a lecture.

"Bill, they're not good company for a young Christian. You told me they swear and tell dirty jokes. You've been a Christian for three years, and I don't understand why you still sit with them."

"Glenda, they welcomed me when I started to work at the plant and taught me everything I know. They covered for my mistakes. I can't turn my back on them now, just because I'm a Christian—like I'm ashamed of them or something."

"Bill, you're not ashamed of them. But when you don't stand up for your faith, you are ashamed of the Lord."

He felt indignant that Glenda said such a thing, but he knew she was right.

"Bill, the Bible says not to be ashamed of the Gospel because it's the power of God for the salvation of everyone who believes

(Romans 1:16 NIV). You can't win them to the Lord if you're ashamed of the same Gospel that saved you."

Her words stirred his heart as he showered before he met his friends at the movie theater.

"Bill, you're a strong enough Christian that this shouldn't bother you, " Tony said when Bill refused to go into the theater.

"This isn't real pornography," Al agreed. "This is just some innocent fun," he said and winked at Chester, who looked embarrassed.

"We paid for these tickets in advance, and I'm staying," Blake said.

Bill looked at Chester, who seemed confused about the whole matter. "Chester, I need to apologize. I realize I've compromised my Christian values many times because I was ashamed to stand up for what I knew was right. I didn't want my friends to feel uncomfortable and think that I was ashamed of them."

His friends avoided his eyes as he spoke.

"The truth is I'm no longer ashamed to act like a Christian. God would not be pleased if I watched this movie, so I'm leaving. But, you're free to do as you wish," he said, smiling at his friends as he left.

"Bill, wait for me!" Chester called out, as he ran to catch up with him.

Are you ashamed to do what's right for fear of rejection? Jesus was rejected yet He gave his life so that you could have access to God. Stand up and be counted for Him.

Lord, You are not ashamed of me in spite of the wrong I've done. I dare not be ashamed of You and Your Gospel that saved me. Amen.

To do what is right and just is more acceptable to the Lord than sacrifice.
PROVERBS 21:3 NIV

It's easy to become a product of your environment.

A GOOD INFLUENCE

HANNAH SMILED PROUDLY AS DEREK AND THE OTHER MEN TALKED. Never in her wildest dreams did she think she would hear her husband contribute to a conversation about God.

This was the same man who, for much of their five years of marriage, had shunned her every effort to talk with him about God.

He sure has changed, Hannah thought. *You can see the love of God all over him.* Since becoming a Christian, Derek had even become particular about the company he kept.

He wanted to learn as much about God as he could, he had told Hannah. "I can't do that hanging around the same old crowd."

The same thing had happened to her as a new Christian, Hannah recalled as she reflected on her own experience. The more time she had spent with other Christians, the more she began to act and talk like them.

She also immersed herself in the Bible, and spent a lot of time praying. Sometimes, her thoughts would go back to the past. But Hannah refused to let thoughts of the past keep her from enjoying what God was doing in her life now. She simply prayed and asked God to help her. She could feel His warm hand on her shoulder, pulling her close to Him as if to say, *think on those things that are good.*

God's love for you is no different. When God created the world, He made man to be just like Him. (Genesis 1:26) That means that you have His nature. The more time you spend with Him, the more you become like Him.

This does not mean you should not spend time with people who are not Christians. These are the very ones that need to hear about God. Just be sure that your habits rub off on them, and not the other way around.

Ever find yourself repeating some of the popular catchphrases of today and wonder: "Where did that come from?" It's because you hang around people who talk like that. When your desire is to please God, you'll make sure you keep company with those who have the same desire.

Father, I always want to be sure my conversation is pure and brings honor to You. That's why I watch the people I associate with. Amen.

*God shows and clearly proves His [own] love for us by the fact that
while we were still sinners, Christ (the Messiah, the Anointed One)
died for us.*
ROMANS 5:8 AMP

The highest result of education is tolerance.

PUT UP
WITH IT

TRACY HAD DECIDED ENOUGH WAS ENOUGH. It was diffi-
cult to share a cubicle in the small insurance office. But to have to sit and
listen to Melanie's constant jabbering on the phone, usually discussing
personal matters, was unbearable.

"I can understand that she has personal problems, and I feel sorry for
her," Tracy told Ashley during a morning break. "But telling everyone
her business will not solve anything. Besides, she hardly gets any work
done anymore. I'm stuck doing the bulk of it."

"I know she'll get upset, but I've been about as patient as I can be.
I'm going to say something to her tomorrow when she comes back from
vacation."

Ashley listened with compassion. But on the inside, she prayed that
God would show her how to respond to Tracy's situation. "Lord, I know
this is not easy for Tracy," she prayed on the way back to her desk. "But
there may be more to Melanie's situation than anyone knows. What can
I do to help both of them?"

In the quiet moments that followed, Ashley thought about Jesus. She remembered how patient and tolerant He was with the disciples during His time with them, despite their seeming inability to understand the things He taught.

She could hear Jesus asking: "How long shall I put up with you?" (Mathew 17:17 NIV) She thought about how Jesus tolerated the crowds, even though they taunted him and tied to kill Him. (John 7:1 NIV) And she remembered that God had loved her so much, that even when she was living in sin He sent Jesus to die for her. (Romans 5:8 NIV)

In her heart, she could hear God saying, *Tell her about my love, and my tolerance.* Ashley decided she would call Tracy later that evening. *She has a good heart, and I know she will understand,* Ashley thought.

Jesus encountered a number of irritations during his time on the Earth. In fact, there was a time when He became angry. But His love for mankind was stronger than the influence of anger. Let the love of God help you exercise patience and tolerance.

Lord, sometimes when I get irritated I speak out before taking the time to think. Help me to be more like you and exercise patience. Amen.

Work hard, but not just to please your masters when they are watching.
EPHESIANS 6:6 NLT

There just isn't any pleasing some people.
The trick is to stop trying.

TRUE ACCEPTANCE

LINDA LOOKED AT HERSELF IN THE MIRROR. *This pretty new dress might give the impression that I am trying to turn some heads in the office,* she thought. Truly Linda had not been seeking attention for herself when she bought the dress.

That would not have been the case a year ago, when the young executive felt her success depended on the approval of others. Acceptance by others had become a top priority with her.

On the surface, Linda appeared to have it all under control. Fresh out of graduate school, she had landed a good-paying job with one of the top accounting firms in the country. She had recently passed the CPA exam, which meant a hefty pay raise and possibly a promotion.

But the way she appeared on the outside was a far cry from what Linda, the product of a broken home, dealt with inwardly. The loss of her best friend to a car accident and then an emotional break-up with her boyfriend had played a major part in Linda's struggle for acceptance.

Living alone with little to no social life only added to her feelings of rejection. But that began to change the day Linda was handed a small religious tract while sitting at a table outside a downtown coffee shop.

"God loves you just as you are, and He wants to be your friend," it read on the front. That night, alone in her small Manhattan apartment, Linda learned about God's love for her as she read from a small Bible her grandmother had given her for graduation. Her heart was touched by the words, which seemed to leap from the pages. It was like God was in the room with her, and speaking directly to her with the words from the Bible.

In the weeks that followed, Linda became a Christian. She had learned what true acceptance was all about. She knew that God's love for her would forever remain unconditional.

When those around you are looking at your outside appearance, God says, "Come as you are." Make sure you want to be accepted for the right reasons.

Lord, I'm glad I don't have to do special things or dress a certain way to get your attention or approval. You accept me as I am, faults and all, and then You help me to get my life in order. I love you so much.
Amen.

Do not worry about anything; instead, pray about everything.
Tell God what you need, and thank him for all he has done.
PHILIPPIANS 4:6 NLT

Blessed is the person who is too busy to worry in the daytime,
and too sleepy to worry at night.

WHAT'S YOUR CONCERN?

IT WAS NOT FUNNY, BUT MICHAEL COULD NOT HELP BUT CHUCKLE ON THE INSIDE AS THE SUPERVISOR EXPLAINED THE ORDEAL.

"We're concerned that we won't make the shipping date again this month," the super had said. "If that happens, it could mean a loss of several thousand dollars."

It was not the matter of missing another deadline that got Michael's attention. It was that word again—CONCERNED! *Why don't they just say what they mean,* Michael thought. *They mean they are worried. They are afraid.*

Words like that had not meant much to Michael in the past. But now that he was a Christian, he paid more attention to the words he used. He wanted to make sure he spoke words that were always encouraging and in line with what God said.

Worry had always been a big part of his life. He worried that he would lose his job. He worried that his car would break down. He even worried that his face would break out in pimples the night before he made a big presentation before a client.

Now, whenever he heard the word "worry," Michael remembered the scripture, "Don't worry." (Philippians 4:6 NLT) Instantly, he pictured God right there with him, saying, *I'll take care of that for you.*

Ask yourself if God saved you so that you could be concerned about things the rest of your life? Would He tell you to come to Him for rest if He intended for you to worry about things?

The answer is no.

So, stop being "concerned." Talk to God about the things that could bring worry. Place them in His capable hands and then leave them there. Once you release them, they're His responsibility. He will be faithful to handle it for you.

There is a saying that people spend most of their time worrying about things that never happen. Whatever you are worried about, God is more than able to handle it. Give it to Him and then trust Him to bring the best possible answer. He will.

Lord, I do worry. And sometimes I get afraid. But I'm leaning on You and trust you to handle those things that I cannot fix anyway. Thank You for being my comfort and my protection. Amen.

*He will take these weak mortal bodies of ours and change them
into glorious bodies like his own, using the same mighty power
that he will use to conquer everything, everywhere.*
PHILIPPIANS 3:21 NLT

God never does things halfway.

A CLEAN
SWEEP

"IT DOESN'T EVEN LOOK LIKE THE SAME PLACE." Whitney
beamed at the sound of those words. The old Victorian house had been
in pretty bad shape when she and Ross bought it six months ago. But
that was okay. As an interior decorator, Whitney loved challenges like
the ones presented by this monstrosity.

Now, her work had paid off, and people noticed it.

Lord, I thank You for guiding me through all of this, Whitney whispered to herself as she showed off her newly-remodeled home to a few
of her friends. *This is your masterpiece, not mine.*

Later that day, Whitney took another walk through the house. This
time, her thoughts were not so much on the ornate draperies in the living room or the brightly lighted chandeliers hanging in the dining room.
She thought about her own life, and the mess it was before God came
in, cleaned it up, and did His own special remodeling.

In her life, everything had been dirty, worn, and tattered. There were
walls scared with anger, floors marred with shame, and windows stained

with guilt. But when she invited God into her life, He became her decorator. Things that had caused hurt and pain were quickly swept away. The anger was replaced with love, shame was exchanged for forgiveness, and the guilt was erased with peace.

Whitney felt brand new as she sensed the presence of God living on the inside of her. She smiled as she looked over her newly remodeled home. It was a welcome compliment to the new home God had created on the inside of her.

There are repairs needed in all of us. But they must be permanent repairs. Only God is capable of fixing us so that we will never break again. Look into your own heart and see where the damage is. Then, invite God to come in and do some permanent repair work. He is a master decorator, so you can be sure it will be done right.

Lord, when I try to fix things I usually botch them. But I know You won't mess things up in my life. I invite You into my heart now, and ask that You make whatever repairs are needed to make me more like Jesus. Amen.

What this means is that those who become Christians become new persons. They are not the same anymore, for the old life is gone. A new life has begun!

II CORINTHIANS 5:17 NLT

Let the potter mold you, just as he would shape a piece of clay—into perfection!

A LIFE CHANGED

TIM TRIED, BUT HE COULDN'T HOLD BACK THE TEARS AS THE PRAISE AND WORSHIP TEAM SANG. "Change my heart, oh God, make me ever new. Change my heart, oh God, let me be like You."

The words were a strong reminder of the troubled life he had lived, and how God had totally transformed him. Sitting in the congregation, Tim had flashbacks of his days as a gang member. He remembered the day he was shot, and thought about what he now knew was a warning from God.

Tim was shot when a drug deal went bad. His assailant had left him for dead. But Tim's life was spared when a passerby saw what looked like a man lying in a culvert and stopped to investigate.

Some people don't believe in angels, Tim thought as he listened to the chorus. *But I know what I saw as I lay there dying.* Tim was also convinced it was God whose hand he felt on his shoulder, comforting him as he struggled to crawl up the hill and to the roadside for help.

Tim spent weeks in the hospital, and months in rehabilitation on his way to recovery. Now, with the help of a cane, he walked. His speech was nearly perfect, and doctors expected him to make a full recovery.

He thought about the mending process his body was going through. *While I was being perfected physically,* he thought, *God had also started renewing my heart.* His life was brand new.

Have you ever seen a warning sign, ignored it, and had to suffer the consequences? God will often warn that there is danger ahead. If you heed that warning, you can avoid the destruction that is waiting.

Lord, when I was lost, confused and headed down the road to destruc-
tion, You came to my rescue. Thank You. Amen.

God is faithful; he will not let you be tempted beyond what you can
bear. But when you are tempted, he will also provide a way out
so that you can stand up under it.
I CORINTHIANS 10:13 NIV

The strength of a man consists in finding out the way God is going,
and going that way.

PUSH TO THE LIMIT

"COME ON, PUSH! PUSH. DON'T STOP NOW! PUSH!"

Tricia was tired. She had been pushing now for hours, and still no baby. She knew it was just a matter of time. And she knew those around her in the delivery room, those shouting encouragement, meant no harm.

They were just as excited that her first baby was about to enter into the world as she was. Still, that didn't make it any easier as she waited and waited, and pushed and pushed. Eventually, there was a baby. And all was well. Tricia had passed the test.

It's a similar experience in the life of a new Christian. At first, you're excited about the expectancy that comes with your new birth. You marvel at how much God has done for you, and you now shun those things that once were a hindrance. But somewhere along the way things begin to get a little tougher. Tests and trials arise that require you to use your faith. Temptation comes and you have to muster up the strength to resist.

God won't let you take on any more than you are strong enough to handle (I Corinthians 10:13). If you have prayed about the matter, it's settled. God knows all about it. He's right there with you, watching to see how you will respond.

Don't quit. Don't give up.

Push until you see the desired results.

What might seem hard for you is never too hard for God. If you're too weak to deal with a matter, you have His strength to draw from. Fight for what's yours. Don't quit.

Thank You, Lord, for giving me strength to stand when times are tough. When I feel weak, I know You are there to make me strong. Amen.

If you are thirsty, come to me!
JOHN 7:37 NLT

A habit of devout fellowship with God is the spring of all our life,
and the strength of it.

AN ALARMING
THIRST

KEN LOOKED UP FROM HIS COMPUTER MONITOR AS THE
ALARM SOUNDED FOR THE THIRD TIME THAT MORNING.

Already, he sensed the presence of God and felt eager to speak with
Him. Pushing the button to reset the timer on his clock, and then reaching for the glass next to a small water dispenser on his desk, he smiled at
the thought of how ridiculous he must look to his coworkers. But that
didn't matter to him. After trying everything else he knew to lose
weight, this new system was paying off.

Not only that, but it had also brought him into a closer relationship
with God. The idea had come to him one morning as Ken read his Bible.
"Those who believe in me will never thirst." (John 6:35 NLT)

Suddenly, Ken had an idea. *That would be a great way for me to get
the water I need, and a point of contact to keep me in constant fellowship
with God,* Ken thought.

The next day at work, Ken placed a small timer next to his computer and a water dispenser nearby. When the timer went off each hour,
Ken drank eight ounces of water and spent a few minutes reading his

Bible.

Although he may not have felt thirsty, the alarm served as a constant reminder to Ken that his body needed water. It also reminded him that his spirit needed refreshment.

Do you have a special time reserved for you and God? With the busyness of the day, finding such time can be difficult. Constant contact with God is a good way to stay nourished on the Word of God. Ask God to help you manage your time so you can have time for Him.

Father, when I pray and read my Bible I have such peace that You are right there with me. Thank You for giving me a hunger and thirst that keep me coming back to Your Word. Amen.

*If his bill runs higher than that, he said,
I'll pay the difference the next time I am here.*
LUKE 10:35 NLT

God has covered every debt you owe.

IT'S BEEN PAID

AMANDA HUNG UP THE PHONE AND SAT QUIETLY ON THE EDGE OF THE BED. It was the third call from a bill collector that morning, and it wasn't even 10 A.M. "Lord, how are we going to pay this bill," Amanda said aloud. "It's bad enough that we can't pay our regular bills. We don't have $14,000 to pay a hospital bill."

Flipping through the pages of itemized charges from her recent hospital stay, Amanda remembered how nice it had been in the first few years of their marriage. She and her husband had good paying jobs, they drove nice cars, and most weeks they ate out at least two or three times.

Since Jessica's premature birth, however, things had changed drastically. Suddenly, there was a mountain of medical bills—brought on by complications Amanda had leading up to Jessica's birth. With Amanda on maternity leave, and not able to return to work because of Jessica's delicate condition, the financial responsibility fell to David.

"Lord, David is a good man and a hard worker," Amanda prayed. "But he can't handle this all alone. We need your help."

Putting the bills aside, Amanda took her Bible from the nightstand

and began to read. "Lord, I see in your Word where You had compassion on this man and forgave him the debt he owed," she said softly. (MATTHEW 18:27 KJV) "Just like you cancelled the debt caused by our sin, I believe you can forgive this debt we owe."

In the quiet of her room, Amanda felt God's peace like a strong arm wrapped around her shoulders. In her heart she could hear Him saying, *Your debt is paid in full.*

Three weeks later, David called to arrange payments on the hospital bill. Amanda knew something unusual had happened by the look on his face. "She said the combined benefit payments from my job and yours were more than enough to cover the bill," David told Amanda. "Where your insurance stopped, mine started. I didn't realize you were covered on both policies. It took awhile to get all the papers processed, but the bill was paid in full three weeks ago."

"I knew you would do it, Lord," Amanda said softly, tears streaming down her face. "You always come through when Your children need you."

Refuse to allow the voice of debt to block God's voice. Pray and ask God to show you how to get out of debt so you can be free to hear His voice.

Lord, it takes wisdom to know how to properly manage finances. I don't have that kind of wisdom, but I know You will give it to me. I thank You for it right now. Amen.

You are already clean because of the word I have spoken to you.
JOHN 15:3 NIV

God removes dirt that no vacuum cleaner can touch.

SQUEAKY CLEAN

MOLLY GROANED AS SHE STOOPED TO WASH THE BOTTOM SHELVES. It was one of the most dreaded of her household chores, but she absolutely could not tolerate a dirty refrigerator.

Molly had commented before that it would sure be nice if someone invented a refrigerator that was self-cleaning. "It doesn't make any sense for a refrigerator to get so dirty so fast," she said to Vince, her husband, who had come into the kitchen for a drink of water.

It's no different than you.

The words caught Molly off guard. At first, she thought it was Vince. Turning to see that her husband had already left the room, Molly then recognized the inner voice of God. He was reminding her about her own cleansing, and how He continued to keep her clean.

Before she became a Christian, Molly's life was stained with the muck of sin. But the Bible tells us that when God comes into your life, He washes away your sin and makes you a new person (II CORINTHIANS 5:17 NIV).

The fact that you are human, and live in a society that is riddled with sin, makes it possible that some of the "dirt" of the world can rub off on you. To stay clean, you must stay close to God, who is the only One able to keep you clean.

To keep the dirt out you have to keep cleaning. That's what God does with you. He puts His word in you so that it will drive out the dirt and keep it out.

Lord, now that You have cleansed me I don't want to become contaminated by the filth of this world. Thank You that I have access to Your Word, which is a cleaning agent for me. Amen.

You, O LORD, are a shield around me, my glory,
and the one who lifts my head high. I cried out to the LORD,
and he answered me from his holy mountain.

PSALM 3:3-4 NLT

A head, once bowed in prayer from indignity,
is now lifted up in compassion and restored to dignity.

BARE
THE PAIN

EMMA HAD CRIED AND PRAYED EVERY DAY SINCE HER EX-FIANCÉE SNUCK OFF WITH HER BEST FRIEND, LEAVING HER WAITING AT THE CHURCH FOR TWO HOURS. *Lord, were they in a horrible accident? Why else wouldn't they be here for our wedding?* her frantic mind had reasoned.

They grew up in the same small town and had been friends since kindergarten. If one was in trouble, they all were. If one was hurt, the other two felt it.

Their families were close, and all of them were angry, confused, and hurt about what happened. But, none so much as Emma. Her parents insisted she stay with them for a month while she tried to make sense of it all. Her sisters encouraged her to get out and talk with friends a little, but she just wasn't quite ready.

After a month, Emma went back to her apartment, against her parents' wishes. She had to face people and get on with her life, but it was easier said than done. She was so embarrassed that she kept her head down and refused to make eye contact. She couldn't stand their pity. She even imagined herself behind a huge shield—protected from anyone ever hurting her again.

One day, her mother said something that touched her heart. "Emma, our Lord was hurt in several ways. First, by His own people who rejected Him. Then, from the excruciating pain and shameful death when they crucified Him. Last of all, as He hung on the Cross, He suffered the emotional agony of being separated from His Heavenly Father."

"The Bible says He is our High Priest and He sympathizes with us because He was hurt and tempted too. He's familiar with hurt and shame. So, we can approach His throne to receive mercy and find grace to help us in our time of need (Hebrews 4:14-16)."

They knelt to pray. For the first time in months, Emma dropped her shield and let God's presence shield her. Then, she lifted her head without shame and looked up to God for His help.

Do you avoid others when you're hurt or feel ashamed? Don't allow your feelings keep you from Your Heavenly Father, whose love is unconditional and who accepts you without reserve.

Lord, help me remember that You are fully aware of my thoughts and feelings. I come to you in confident trust when I'm hurt or ashamed, knowing that You understand and no explanations are necessary.
Amen.

He was pierced for our transgressions, he was crushed for our iniquities; the punishment that brought us peace was upon him, and by his wounds we are healed.
ISAIAH 53:5 NIV

Pains of love be sweeter far than all the other pleasures are.

A PIERCING STATEMENT

"Ouch, that hurt!" Monica screamed.

"Oh, stop being such a baby," Heather told her.

Monica fought back the tears as the sharp needle pierced her left ear. But the pain the second time around was almost more than she could stand.

"I'm sorry, girl, but that hurt," she told Heather later. "You must be a lot tougher than me if it didn't bother you. I don't know why I waited until I was twenty-five to get my ears pierced."

"I didn't say it didn't hurt," Heather said laughingly. "Actually, I even cried when I got my ears pierced. But it wasn't just because of the pain I felt."

"What do you mean?"

"I cried because of Jesus," Heather answered. "I thought about what He must have gone through when He was nailed to the Cross."

That evening, Heather reflected on her conversation with Monica as she examined her freshly pierced earlobes. She pictured Jesus nailed to a cross, and tried to imagine the pain He must have felt from the sharp nails. Then, she remembered how peaceful she felt on the inside when she asked Jesus to come into her heart. It was like He was right there with her, with His arms around her shoulders. The stinging pain from her ears left as Monica felt that same peace again.

"Lord, You must have loved me a lot to be willing to suffer such pain," she whispered softly. "I will remember that love every time I look at my own piercing."

Body piercing.

Ears, tongues, navels.

It's everywhere you look.

But what does it represent?

The piercing that Jesus endured was like none man will ever face.

Though they caused Him pain, Jesus endured the nails in His hands and feet because of His love for mankind.

It was His way of saying, "I love you."

No one enjoys pain. Unfortunately, there are times when it comes. When you feel pain, look to God to provide relief. He understands pain, and stands ready to comfort you.

Lord, there are times when I hurt and don't know what to do. Thank You for showing me that You know what real pain is, and You will be my comfort. Amen.

He was . . . a Man of sorrows and pains,
and acquainted with grief and sickness . . . . He has borne our griefs
(sicknesses, weaknesses and distresses) and carried our sorrows and
pains.
ISAIAH 53:3-4 AMP

Sharing the hurt makes it lighter; bearing the hurt makes it go away.

MAKE IT
GO AWAY!

That was Tammy! Sharon clicked on the dishwasher and ran to the front door when she heard the piercing scream. Tammy, her eight-year-old, was crying as she looked at the blood on her scraped knees. Her new bicycle, its wheels bent, was beside her on the driveway.

"Mommy, it hurts real bad!" she cried. Sharon picked her up in her arms and carried her to the bathroom.

"Mommy, make it stop hurting!" Sharon seemed to feel Tammy's pain as she washed her knees, applied an antibiotic cream and bandaged them.

Still whimpering, Tammy limped to the front door and saw her damaged bike. She burst into fresh sobs. She realized her disobedience disappointed and hurt her mother. And on top of that, the pretty new bike she received for her birthday was damaged.

"I'm so sorry I didn't do what you told me," she confessed as she hugged her mom. "Please forgive me."

Sharon returned her hug and told her she was forgiven. She assured her that her life was much more important than the bike's bent wheels. Sharon let Tammy know that the wheels could be replaced, but her life could not.

She made Tammy a peanut butter and jelly sandwich, and poured a glass of milk and then set her in front of her favorite video. Then, she returned to the kitchen to start preparations for dinner and make a salad for her lunch. As Sharon cut the tomatoes, she thought about what just happened with Tammy and her bike.

Tammy's disobedience hurt her and her mother, and damaged her bike. Sharon went to her side to comfort her as soon as she heard her cry. She picked her up and cleaned her wounds. She eased her emotional pain by letting her know her life was more important than the bike's bent wheels.

When Tammy admitted her disobedience and asked forgiveness, Sharon immediately forgave her and promised to have her bike repaired. "Lord, the compassion, love, and forgiveness I showed Tammy is an excellent example of Your love to us. I did my best to make her hurt, sorrow, and guilt go away. Even my promise to repair her bike is like Your promise to us of a new life.

The sound of Tammy's giggles let Sharon know her pain had gone away. "Lord, thank You for Your wonderful love and for this perfect lesson of Your love."

Do you sometimes wish that the emotional and physical pain and suffering would go away? Give all of it to God who has the strength to carry it.

Lord, thank You for Your love and compassion that make You so willing to carry my hurt and sorrow. Amen.

The LORD your God is with you, ...He will take great delight in you, . . . he will rejoice over you with singing.

ZEPHANIAH 3:17 NIV

Such songs have power to quiet
The restless pulse of care,
And come like the benediction
That follows after prayer.

MUSIC IN THE AIR

CHELSEA FELT HER HEART SWELL WITH JOY AS SHE PRAISED GOD WITH THE REST OF THE CHOIR. Music had always been her passion. It began when she was a little girl and sang along with her parents' old records. Next came voice and piano lessons, and then the school choir.

During high school, she was in the concert band and choir. She won numerous awards and received a scholarship for college.

After graduation, she taught music appreciation at a local middle school. Students initially thought her class would be the opportune time to doze or socialize, but they were mistaken. She taught music in such an exciting way that even the most ardent rap and hip-hop music lovers learned to appreciate opera and classical music.

She had married Paul, a music professor at their alma mater and they had four children. Naturally, their home was filled with squawks, squeaks and thunderous booms coming from different instruments, as each child tried to find their own music niche. Chelsea would just laugh and say, "There's music in the air."

Tragedy struck their family when Chelsea suffered a stroke. Her beautiful voice was quieted, but the joy in her eyes shone when family, students, and choir members visited and played their instruments or sang for her. Therapy was hard and recuperation was slow, but her family constantly encouraged her with music.

One night, Chelsea heard the most melodious sound—like someone singing far above her. She sensed that God was singing just for her because He knew how much she missed praising Him with her own voice. It happened often, and each melody was different. She began trying to hum with the melodies. Paul never stirred.

Chelsea's doctors were amazed as she began to improve miraculously each week. Within a few months, she was sitting in Sunday services. Soon, she was brought to choir rehearsals. She began voice training again, and two years later, was back on the choir. Her voice was stronger and more beautiful than it had ever been.

The beautiful melodies kept coming, but not as frequently. Chelsea began playing them on her piano. Years later, her grandchildren scrambled to get a seat on the sofa when she played those special melodies—Grandma's "special music in the air" songs.

Humbly receive the songs your Heavenly Father sings over you. Thank Him that He has found such delight in you.

Lord, thank You for finding such delight in me that causes You to sing over me. I pray that You delight in the songs I sing to You about Your goodness. Amen.

*"Come to me, all of you who are weary and carry heavy burdens,
and I will give you rest."*
MATTHEW 11:28 NLT

Rest refreshes the soul and body.

TIME OUT!

"MARCUS, YOU'RE OVERLOADED. YOU'RE ABOUT TO BURN OUT," DR. WARREN SAID IN A FIRM VOICE. "The same thing that happens to an overloaded circuit is going to happen to you if you don't get some much-needed rest." He closed Reverend Simon's medical folder and looked him in the eye.

"Doc," his dear friend said, "you and I have been trying to save lives and souls a long time. We both know rest is a luxury we can't afford because our duties never end. Try as we might, lives still might end," he said sorrowfully, "but our duties do not."

Dr. Warren looked at the lines of weariness in his friend's thin face. His temples appeared to have become grayer since his last visit. His eyes didn't have the sparkle they used to have. And his shoulders drooped as if he carried the weight of the world.

"Marcus, Rebecca wouldn't want you to wear yourself out like this. You know how she made such a fuss when you didn't take care of yourself. Besides, you've got your children and grandchildren to think of. And, God only knows what will happen to your parishioners if you aren't there to sing Amazing Grace on Sunday mornings."

Reverend Simons chuckled as he remembered how his dear wife would mouth to him, "Please don't sing," when his trembling voice started his favorite hymn.

"I miss her so much, Doc. Even when she was very sick, she didn't pity herself. She wouldn't let me take the time to care for her because she said too many other lives depended on me."

Lord, thank You for giving him this opportunity to pour out his heart. He's made himself available for so many others, Doc prayed silently.

"If things got too hard," Reverend Simmons continued, "she was always there to share the load. When I didn't feel like I could take another step, she took my hand and helped me. She even insisted I nap on Saturdays. She did everything she could to make it easy for me so I could get some . . ."

He stopped when he saw the *Now, you're finally catching on!* look on his doctor's face.

" . . . rest," he finished, with an embarrassed look.

"Marcus, you need to rest your mind and your body. If Rebecca was so willing to help you rest, how much more willing and able is your Heavenly Father?"

He took Reverend Simmons' hand and began to pray, "Heavenly Father, Your servant and my friend needs rest . . . ."

Weariness burdens your mind and your body. It makes the simplest thing seem difficult. Your Heavenly Father desires for you to totally rest in Him.

Lord, help me learn to rest in You. Show me how to live so weariness doesn't hinder me from carrying out Your will. Amen.

When you do something for someone else,
don't call attention to yourself. . . . When you help someone out, don't
think about how it looks. Just do it—quietly and unobtrusively.
MATTHEW 6: 2-4 MSG

Let what you do to help others speak for itself.

JUST
BETWEEN US

Andrew saw holes in the bottoms of Frank's shoes as they sat in church. He noticed the shine on Frank's pants that could only come from numerous washings and repeated ironing, and an odd button was sewn on his faded shirt.

Wendy, Frank's wife, wore no make-up, her shaggy ponytail was bound with a rubber band, and the hem of her black dress was tacked up with red thread. None of that hindered their joy and enthusiasm as they sang with the choir.

Frank and Wendy had accepted Christ six months ago and were so excited and happy about their new lives that they hadn't missed a service. That evening, Andrew and his wife, Stella, prayed for the Lord to show them how they could help Frank and Wendy. They sensed His answer right away.

The next Saturday Andrew and Stella spent the day chauffeuring Frank and Wendy from mall to mall. In one of the stores, unbeknownst to Andrew and Stella, Mrs. Chambers, a long-time church member, spotted them and overheard Andrew tell the cashier to add the charge to their monthly bill.

On Sunday morning Mrs. Chambers approached Stella in the restroom. She applauded Andrew and Stella for having pity on Frank and Wendy—the "poor things". She went on and on about how they had "spent their own hard-earned money for such expensive clothes when the church benevolence fund should have taken care of them." Mrs. Chambers suggested they could have bought something at a second-hand store that would have looked just as nice. Then she proceeded to say that Frank and Wendy would have been thankful anyway.

Stella smiled and said, "It's a pleasure to bless others and we choose not to talk about it to anyone." Mrs. Chambers ignored her as she rushed to be the first to tell a friend who had come in what Andrew and Stella had done. As soon as Mrs. Chambers and her friend left, Wendy came out of a stall.

Stella apologized to Wendy for the comments she had heard.

Wendy smiled and said, "No apology is necessary. You helped us without bragging on yourselves. Someone else saw what you did for us and bragged about you," she smiled.

It's easy to become excited and want to tell someone what you did for another. God wants to hear all about it. Tell your Heavenly Father how much you appreciate the privilege to bless someone.

Lord, You only wanted others to know what You did for them for God's glory—not Yours. Help me be humbly grateful to You that I'm able to bless others. Amen.

Pray for each other . . . . The earnest prayer of a righteous person has great power and wonderful results.
JAMES 5:16 NLT

And, when I pray, my heart is in my prayer.

SOMEONE IS PRAYING

REVEREND PRINCETON GAVE THE BENEDICTION AND DISMISSED THE SMALL CONGREGATION. As he drove out of his reserved parking space, he remembered the many requests from the church members for prayer.

"Reverend, please pray . . . ." accompanied almost every handshake.

"Well, Heavenly Father, I guess now is as good a time as any to get started, but I'm relying on Your Spirit to bring the names and their particular requests to my remembrance. You know just how to do it."

He patiently prayed as the Holy Spirit brought each name and request to his heart and mind. When he pulled into his garage, he remembered Sam who needed another car. When he turned the key in the lock, he thought about a family whose house was foreclosed. When he walked into his living room, he thought about a family who had lost their belongings in a house fire.

Myra, his wife, greeted him in the kitchen where she had prepared his favorite meal. This reminded him of the church's food bank whose provisions were seriously low.

The pictures of his children on the fireplace mantel reminded him to pray for a couple whose children were on drugs. His wife's beautiful wedding portrait prompted him to pray for Ben, whose dear wife of 60 years had died.

As he showered, he remembered Don who had suffered a stroke and was in physical therapy. Finally, when he and Myra got in bed, a few couples that were going through divorce came to his mind. As he was about to drift to sleep, he remembered he hadn't prayed for his own family.

"Lord, forgive me for neglecting to pray for my own family," he whispered as got on his knees. As he began to pray, he sensed the Lord reminding him that just as he'd prayed for others, others were praying for his family.

"Heavenly Father, thank You for Your built-in security system of prayer. It's great knowing you've got our backs covered."

As you spend time talking to God, don't worry about the requests that you forgot. Your Heavenly Father has a network of prayer that covers you and your family.

Lord, help me to be ready to pray for anyone at any time. Thank You for the assurance that You have someone doing the same for my family. Amen.

Be quiet and at ease, . . . 'For I am with you', declares the LORD.
JEREMIAH 30:10-11 NASB

Quietness is to peace like loudness is to confusion.

SHH!
BE QUIET!

MISTI LAUGHED AT THE NOISY, HAPPY KINDERGARTEN-ERS AS THEY ROMPED AND PLAYED ON THE PLAYGROUND.

"Thank you, Lord, that they are healthy and happy enough to be noisy and even get in trouble," she laughed as Michael tugged at Nikki's braids.

She glanced at her watch. Only fifteen more minutes and then she would have to corral them back inside. If it were left up to her, she would keep them out longer. "But, rules are rules, and they are for their good," she conceded. She blew her whistle to get their attention and let them know it was time to go inside.

Once inside, Misti gently but firmly reminded them they weren't outside anymore and they slowly adjusted themselves accordingly. She let them wash their hands and have a snack and some juice. Then they took a bathroom break and settled down for a quiet story and a nap.

By the time Misti finished the story, they were all peacefully sleeping.

Misti remembered the call that morning from her mother who lived 700 miles away. Her mother was upset and in tears as she told Misti the latest family troubles, quarrels, injustices, and hurt feelings. At first, Misti felt aggravated that her mother brought her into situations that she had absolutely nothing to do with. She felt frustrated because she wanted to relieve her mother's distress.

In her quiet time before class that morning, just as she was about to voice her own feelings, she heard God say to her heart, *Shh! Just be quiet. I understand and I'll take care of it. It will be all right. You'll see.*

Misti telephoned her mother and calmly told her what God said to her. After an hour, her mother's tears had turned into a few sniffles. Then they prayed. Before they hung up, her mother had quieted and was even chuckling about some of the silly things Misti's Uncle Bob had done.

Slight snoring brought Misti's attention back to her classroom. She gave a contented sigh and picked up her Bible to read while she enjoyed the quiet.

Do you desire to pull aside from the loud hustle and bustle of everyday life that is clamoring for your attention? Your Heavenly Father will help you tune in to His blessed quiet so that you can tune out the confusion around you.

Lord, help me turn to You when everything around me is so loud and so busy that I can hardly hear my own thoughts. From my heart I desire Your quietness so I can hear Your voice. Amen.

Let us seize and hold fast and retain without wavering the hope
we cherish and confess . . . for He Who promised is reliable (sure) and
faithful to His word.
HEBREWS 10:23 AMP

If you live the truth loud enough,
then your soft-spoken word will still be heard.

YOU PROMISED!

LOGAN KEPT LOOKING AT HIS WATCH WHILE HE FINISHED WRITING HIS REPORT. "Lord", he quietly prayed, "I don't know why You urged me to do this on the plane when I told Mr. Stiles I'd have it ready first thing when I returned. But, I'm smart enough to know that You know what's best."

His plane would be landing in an hour. He would have just enough time to rush home and put luggage and fishing gear in the truck before Timmy, his 10-year-old, climbed off the school bus.

Logan had planned this trip last spring so he and Timmy could have some time together. Janet, his wife, agreed to remain at home. In fact, Timmy proudly told his mother that just the "men" could go this time. Janet stifled her laughter and tried to look disappointed when he said it.

Logan greeted Janet with a tight hug and long kiss before he went upstairs to get his and Timmy's luggage. Then, he went to the garage to get their fishing gear. While Janet packed their lunch for the drive to the lake, the phone rang. With a somber look, she grudgingly handed it to Logan. Her look warned Logan to brace himself.

His boss' secretary apologized for the interruption, but said Mr. Stiles needed Logan's business report right now. *Now, I know why You led me to finish that report on the plane. Thank You, Lord.*

At that moment, Timmy got off the school bus and rushed through the door. His huge grin faded when he heard Logan's conversation. Disappointed, he forced a smile, hugged his dad, and turned to go upstairs.

"Carol, please tell Mr. Stiles that my wife will bring you the report in about forty-five minutes. I promised my son that we would take a week of much needed R&R, and we've got to get on the road before dark. I'll see you in about ten days."

"Dad, you did what you promised just like you told me God keeps His promise," Timmy said as he helped his father load their supplies into the truck.

What greater testimony than to hear someone say about you, "Whatever they say, you can depend on it. They keep their word." When you listen to God, He'll help you keep promises like He keeps to you.

Lord, thank You that Your promises are truth. Your Word never falters or fails. That is why I place my life in Your hands. Amen.

ACKNOWLEDGEMENTS

Franklin D. Roosevelt (6, 100), James Cash Penney (8), Anonymous (10, 20, 24, 34, 38, 42, 52, 70, 74, 84, 92, 106, 108, 124, 130, 132, 134, 136, 144, 146, 148, 150, 160, 162, 164, 166, 168, 176, 178, 184, 186, 188, 192, 196, 198, 202, 204) Hubert H. Humphrey (12), Dale Carnegie (14), Abraham Lincoln (16, 80), Martin Luther King, Jr. (18, 114), Charles Dickens (22), James Russell Lowell (26, 90), Barbara Bush (28), Mark Twain (30, 62), T. S. Eliot (32), Edward S. Martin (36), Pope John Paul II (40), Julia C. R. Dorr (44), Benjamin Franklin (46, 122), Henry Wadsworth Longfellow (48, 88, 194, 200), Charles A. Dana (50), Justice Oliver Wendell Holmes (54), Kahlil Gibran (56, 142), Henry Adams (58), Amos Bronson Alcott (60), Emerson (64, 138, 154), Park Benjamin (66), Dwight D. Eisenhower (68), Louisa May Alcott (72), Althea Gibson (76), Malcolm Forbes (78), Lew Wallace (82), Arthur Guiterman, (86), Phillips Brooks (94), Henry Ward Beecher (96, 180), Herbert Hoover (98), Will Rogers (102), William Lloyd Garrison (104), Reginald Wright Kauffman (110), Washington Irving (112), Daniel Webster (116), Thomas Jefferson (118), Norman Thomas (120), Michel de Montaigne (126), Mary Brown (128), John Greenleaf Whittier (140), Henry D. Thoreau (152), Dwight L. Moody (156), Ivern Ball(158), Helen Keller (170), Joel Rosenberg (172), Leo Aikman (174), Henry Edward Manning (182), John Dryden (190).

Additional copies of this
and other titles from Honor Books
are available from your local bookstore.

God's Hand on My Shoulder for Women
God's Hand on My Shoulder for Teens

If you have enjoyed this book,
and if it has had an impact on your life,
we would like to hear from you.

Please contact us at:

Honor Books
An Imprint of Cook Communications Ministries
4050 Lee Vance View
Colorado Springs, Colorado 80918
Or visit us online at: www.cookministries.com

Inspiration and Motivation for the Season of Life